Women in Architecture

Women in Architecture

Past, Present, and Future

Ursula Schwitalla (Ed.)

Contents

Foreword

Since 1987, the lecture series "Architecture Today" at the University of Tübingen has offered architects from all over the world a forum to present their work and ideas on building culture. Critics and theorists are also invited to hold lectures on the topic of the current semester or one that is relevant in their particular country. All of this takes place at a university that does not have a faculty of architecture.

As an outstanding informative event for architects, art historians, and a large audience interested in culture, the lecture series quickly gained a reputation beyond the immediate region. It is organized by Ursula Schwitalla, an art historian from Tübingen and associate member of the Association of German Architects (BDA), who has been planning and organizing the event for many years with great commitment on behalf of the Institute of Art History, the Tübinger Kunstgeschichtliche Gesellschaft, the regional district groups of the Chamber of Architects, and the BDA. The continuity of the lecture series is also due to the long-standing and generous financial support of the Sto Foundation. Many internationally renowned figures in the world of architecture, among them ten Pritzker Prize winners—including two of only four female winners of this prize to date—have presented their projects in Tübingen.

For many years there has also been a need to give visionary female architects and urban planners a voice, which led to the publication *Women in Architecture,* which is now available here. It follows on the widely acclaimed publication from 2007 entitled *Built or Unbuilt: Architects Present Their Favorite Projects,* which, as the title suggests, presents the favorite projects—built or not—of the architects participating in the lecture series.

In the two winter semesters of 2016/17 and 2017/18, only women architects were invited to give lectures. In addition to the lecturers who had already presented in Tübingen in previous years, we may now benefit from the extremely enlightening insights into the current work and ideas of thirty-six women architects. The publication once again shows the high level of professional competence and extraordinary commitment of women, and, above all, their highly personal contribution to architecture, a field that has been largely dominated by men until now. The selection of women architects and their projects is based on this series of lectures, which is why, of course, no claim can be made to completeness.

As an introduction to the contemporary representatives, a look at the current situation of women in architecture, and a review of the pioneers in professional practice complement this documentation. Four individual chapters are also dedicated to the work and achievements of outstanding women architects in the past and present. Important role models for the younger generation of women architects include Emilie Winkelmann with the Leistikowhaus in Berlin, Eileen Gray and her E.1027 in Roquebrune-Cap-Martin, Lina Bo Bardi with her Glass House in São Paulo, and last but not least, Zaha Hadid and her exuberant innovative power.

We would like to thank Ursula Schwitalla as well as the authors and architects who have made their projects available and thus made possible an informative *promenade architecturale* through international building culture.

Ernst Seidl

Professor, Institute of Art History, University of Tübingen
Director, Museum of the University of Tübingen (MUT)
Chairperson of the Board, Tübinger Kunstgeschichtliche Gesellschaft e.V. (TGK)

Being a Woman in the Architectural Field

Odile Decq

This book is a step on a long path, carried out by Ursula Schwitalla in the lecture series "Architecture Today" to finally give women in architecture a voice. This book is a window for hope in our field, where we are still underrepresented today, even in 2020. It creates confidence that women can be successful in this field and will encourage young women to take up this wonderful profession.

I have been an architect for nearly forty years and yet recall very well two crucial moments as a budding architect that confronted me with discrimination against women in architecture. When I announced to my parents that I had passed the entrance exam to study architecture, my father said to me that it was no profession for women, and that I should instead become an interior designer or take up a more feminine profession. He invited an architect friend of his to dinner and in response to his question, "little Mademoiselle, why do you want to become an architect?" I responded that I wanted to build a theater. Why I said theater, I don't know, and I have yet to build one today. He was quite shocked by my response and after a moment of silence he turned to my father and said: "It is good that young women want to become architects today, because they are much more pragmatic in their thinking than men and will design cabinets and kitchens very efficiently!" I was furious. After his departure, I told my parents that this man was a jerk and then I left! I studied architecture anyway, first two years in Rennes and then in Paris.

The second crucial moment happened a year after receiving my diploma in Paris, when I was supposed to take an oath to join the chamber of architects. The room was full of young architects—but all of them were men. I immediately realized that it would be a struggle to gain acceptance in this male-dominated field.

After I completed my studies in the late nineteen-seventies, there was not a lot of work for young architects; nevertheless, I immediately became independent and never worked for another architect, even if that meant that I frequently had only sandwiches and potatoes to eat. In 1985, with Benoît Cornette, I cofounded the architectural firm ODBC, which we ran together for nearly fifteen years. After his death, people advised me to close the office and work for another architect rather than continue to run it alone as a woman. At the time, there was a whole generation of architectural firms in which the women remained invisible behind the male head of the office. They ran the office, but they were never present at meetings with the clients and were not represented in the firm's name. Today, women architects often work in an office partnership or as part of a group, and their names are certainly present, but only a few of them establish their own office.

I continued to run the office and changed the name only after journalists wrote that my success was indebted to the collaboration of my deceased partner—for example, in the competition for the MACRO museum in Rome, even though I won it two years after his death!

I have been running Studio Odile Decq alone for more than twenty years. Today, I no longer complain. I am not angry at men in architecture—even though I still occasionally get appalling remarks from them. As women, we are declared hysterical when we make firm demands, whereas men are considered strong for the same reason! But, my enthusiasm for designing and building projects, buildings, objects, and much more dominates.

Since the early nineteen-nineties, I have not only been a practicing architect but have also taught architecture. Fifteen years later, I was chosen to be the director of the École Spéciale d'Architecture (ESA) and in that function tried to develop the school, until several of the long-established members of the faculty made my life so difficult that I resigned in

2012. On the day of my resignation, as I drank a glass of wine with friends, I was asked whether I wanted to found a new school for architecture. I worked on it for two years, creating the education program, the nature of the teaching, and the organization of the school, and in September 2014 the Confluence Institute for Innovation and Creative Strategies in Architecture was launched. Six years later, we are still alive and well. I really enjoy meeting students who are smiling when I arrive.

I often talk to female students in the school and encourage them to be more self-confident. This is a problem women often have: not being self-confident enough to trust themselves to be able architects. We often say that women have to be twice or three times as competent as men to reach the same position, and this is still true today. Even so, women often doubt their ability to succeed.

It is a question of education, from their family and from the society around them. Mothers too often love their sons and ask their daughters to help them. Fathers too often admire the beauty and docility of their daughters while praising the strength and courage of their sons. It's a shame: the starting point is not equal. I continue to observe these patterns even with young, modern couples today!

While nearly 60 percent of students today are women, we find that only around 10 percent of the architects leading an office are women. Where are the other 50 percent of the architecture students? Where do they go and what do they become? The quiet wife standing behind her man? The quiet but efficient office worker paid only 70 percent of the normal salary? What is even stranger is the fact of private schools, because this is not the same average. I had noticed this before in my post as director of the ESA. I asked the students if they knew the reason why. Some of them answered that they had to fight with their parents —in particular their fathers—to be able to study in a private school where they were required to

pay tuition instead of going to a public one. One father didn't want to spend money for his daughter to study architecture because he said that she would never become an architect. When she insisted on studying architecture anyway, he answered that the public school was open to her! In my new little private school, this is the same: 40 percent are women, instead of the 60 percent found elsewhere.

So, we need to help young women to study architecture when and where they want to; we need to put a stop to new surveys like the one that says one woman architect in five will never recommend that a young woman study architecture. This is problematic as a new tendency.

If we want to modify that situation, we need to reconsider architecture studies and stop considering them solely as professional studies that only bring students to work in architectural firms. Architecture education must provide more opportunities for working in diverse situations, including those off the beaten track. The skills of the discipline of architecture are so complete and so wide. To be educated in architecture gives you a specific attitude towards acting in the world. We are able to face highly complex problems, to analyze them; we are able to think on multiple scales simultaneously—from the very small to the very large. We are able to diagnose problems and propose a single solution. We are problem solvers. So, by crossing architectural studies with other disciplines facing society today, by considering the global more than the specific in education, we can help students—and women in particular—to decide the course of their own life, their own way of practicing architecture without being only an architect. We need to rethink and rebuild the curriculum of the studies; we need to help them to become autonomous and self-confident. I strongly believe it is possible and this is what I try to do for the future.

Women in the History of Architecture

Ursula Schwitalla

The history of architecture has hardly any women's names at all. A lack of access to education and the barring of their acceptance into the profession are the reasons that even today the number of documented works by women architects is limited. Scholars have not paid much attention to the women who managed to practice architecture despite these obstacles. For that reason, it seems all the more important today to look at women in the history of architecture in order to expand historical research. Doing so is one of the intentions of this publication.[1]

In the Middle Ages, the profession of architecture as we know it today, as the combination of the planning and execution of a building, did not yet exist. The tasks were instead divided between three authorities: the founder or client, the building administrator (*Bauverwalter*), and the master of the craft (*Werkmeister*), all of whom were integrated into the masons' guilds and learned their craft there through practical activity, sample books, and an oral tradition. Training as master of the craft was reserved exclusively for men. Nor were women allowed to join the guilds that organized and exchanged architects in Europe into the nineteenth century. Women appear as architects at most as widows, who had to remarry within two years of the death of their husbands or lose the business.

The early textbooks on architecture were anthologies of examples of ancient buildings, including the only surviving book on architecture from antiquity, *Ten Books on Architecture* by Vitruvius;[2] Leon Battista Alberti's early modern treatise on architecture;[3] and Andrea Palladio's books on the history of architecture.[4] In principle, therefore, there were textbooks available in Europe that were accessible to privileged women, but they were not yet accepted as practicing architects. There are individual examples of women documented as working as architects and site managers for the first time on the construction of monasteries in Europe during the modern era.[5] In no case, however, is their authorship documented, since

what mattered to these anonymous women architects was not artistic fame but the application of spiritual goals in architecture.

The modern history of the academy—the precursor of our colleges and universities today—begins in the second half of the seventeenth century as a learned association. Based on the ancient model, intellectual men met and exchanged ideas. Women were excluded from these circles. These evolved into the academies of the arts, where architecture was, however, subordinated to *disegno* (drawing), the mother of all arts.

The first academy of architecture in France, founded in 1671 under Louis XIV, offered only instruction in theory and had been established as a kind of building inspection authority and arbiter of taste.[6] Ultimately, as a consequence of the strict separation of art and technology, the Bauakademie (Academy of Architecture) became independent of the Akademie der Künste (Academy of the Arts) in Berlin in 1799. Here too, however, the competing self-images of the creative artist-architect, on the one hand, and the engineer-architect, on the other, manifested themselves. Both could be used to justify excluding women from this profession.

In 1794, at the recently established École polytechnique and later at the École des Beaux-Arts in Paris, the first program for studying architecture was established in Paris. Twenty years later, polytechnic colleges based on that model, which taught both theory and practice, were established in other European countries. Until the beginning of the next century, women were not granted access to study. One exception was the Polytechnikum (now Eidgenössische Technische Hochschule) in Zurich: women were admitted there from 1855 onward.[7] Only women from abroad could take advantage of that offer, however, because Swiss women lacked the required degree from a secondary school, to which they did not have access at the time.[8] Only in the wake of

A construction worker above the rooftops of Berlin, ca. 1910

the emergent women's movement in Europe and the United States in the nineteenth and twentieth centuries, in which women fought for civil rights, equal treatment under the law, the right to education, the right to work, and the right to free choice of a profession, could women in other countries gradually gain access to architectural education and official permission to practice the profession.

Katherine Briçonnet (1494–1526): Lady of the Castle and Construction Manager

The wife of Thomas Bohier, the lord of Château de Chenonceau on the Loire River, supervised the construction site for the new building when her husband was absent and designed a stairway leading directly to the upper story, which was a striking innovation at the time, since spiral staircases had been usual previously.[9] Her pride in her work is evident from the inscription above the door to the front courtyard: "S'il vient à point, me souviendra" (If it is built, I will be remembered). Her two successors, Diane de Poitiers and Catherine de' Medici, also instigated and supervised architectural changes to the castle.

Plautilla Bricci (1616–1705): "Architettrice"

The name of the first professional woman architect appears in Rome in the seventeenth century: Plautilla Bricci. She came from a family of artists and was trained by her father as a painter. Her great supporter in Rome was abbot Elpidio Benedetti, who worked as an art agent for the court of Louis XIV. Benedetti, who was himself interested in architecture, commissioned forty-eight-year-old Plautilla Bricci to design a villa in Rome.[10] Four years later, her elegant but conventional villa was finished. The coat of arms of the Bourbons was placed in the center of the facade as a dedication to Louis XIV. The client published, under the pseudonym Matteo Mayer, a description of the building in 1677 as well as an engraving of the facade facing the Via Aurelia.[11] Astonishingly, there Benedetti attributes the design of the architecture to the architect's brother, even though there is documentation that he later entrusted to Bricci the design of other buildings, such as the chapel of Saint Louis in the church San Luigi dei Francesi in Rome. He was following the social norm of the time that did not wish to acknowledge that a woman could be an architect.

Elizabeth Wilbraham (1632–1705): The Autodidact

Born into the English aristocratic Mytton family, Elizabeth, Lady Wilbraham, designed her own country house in the Palladian style in 1671.[12] She owned several books on architecture, including the first volume of Palladio's *Quattro libri*, which contains her handwritten notes. On her honeymoon journey through Europe, she studied the buildings of the Baroque architect Pieter Post in the Netherlands and Palladio's in Italy, which enabled her to expand her

Katherine Briçonnet, lady of the Château de Chenonceau, on the tapestry *La Danse*, ca. 1500, 220 × 319 cm (detail)

Elizabeth Wilbraham, painting by Peter Lely, 17th century, oil on canvas, 125.7 × 99 cm

Plautilla Bricci, Villa Benedetti, design of the western side facade with three stories, window openings, and arcade facing the garden, drawing 1663

Plautilla Bricci, Villa Benedetti, facade above the artificial stone base to the Via Aurelia, copperplate engraving from the author's description of the villa under the pseudonym Matteo Mayer: Villa Benedetti, 1677

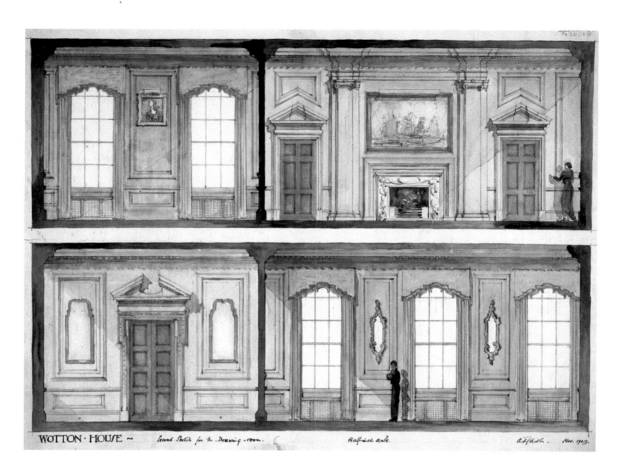

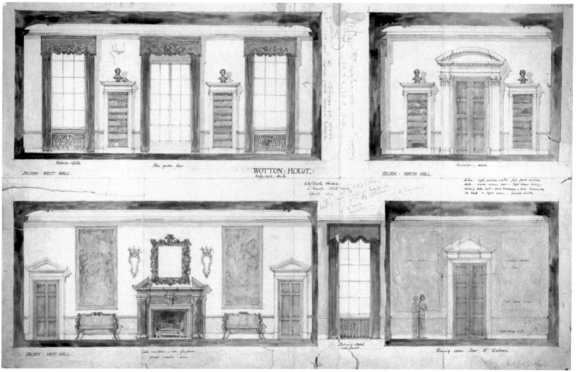

Elizabeth Wilbraham, Wotton House, elevation of the salon walls, watercolor by A. S. G. Butler, 1929. Wotton House, built between 1704 and 1714 in Buckinghamshire, is an important testimony to the English Baroque period attributed to Elizabeth Wilbraham. Destroyed by fire, it was rebuilt in 1820 according to the original design with the sliding windows she preferred.

Louise Blanchard Bethune, Hotel Lafayette, Buffalo, NY, built in 1904 in the neo-Renaissance style. All rooms were equipped with hot and cold running water and a telephone, a highly progressive measure at the time.

Signe Hornborg, residence in Pori, Finland, built in 1892 in the neo-Renaissance style and named "Signellina" after the architect.

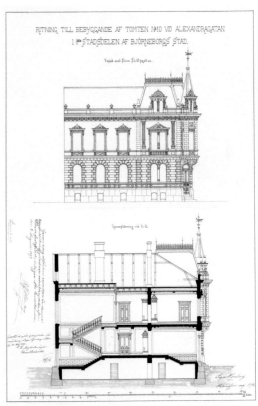

"Signellina," elevation and section, original drawing 1892

Louise Blanchard Bethune

Signe Hornborg

great interest in and knowledge of architecture. It is reasonable to assume that she designed other buildings for her family, including Wotton House in Buckinghamshire and many small churches in the region. Even though her name is not documented in the plans, Dutch and Italian influences in the buildings hint at her authorship of the buildings that have been attributed to her.[13] Because, as a woman, she could not formally present herself as an architect, she had to hire male architects to manage construction. For that reason, her name as an architect long remained in obscurity. In his most recent research, the American cultural historian John Millar now assumes that Wilbraham not only worked with Christopher Wren (1632–1723), the most important English architect of the time, but even worked as a tutor for him and influenced his designs.[14]

Louise Blanchard Bethune (1856–1913): Independent Practice

At the age of twenty-five, Louise Blanchard Bethune opened her own architectural firm in Buffalo, New York, in 1881, and seven years later she was accepted as the first woman member of the American Institute of Architects (AIA).[15] She was from a Huguenot family and became interested in architecture as a teenager. Two years after finishing school, she was preparing to attend Cornell University, which had just opened, but then decided not to study and instead to work as a draftswoman in an architectural office in Buffalo, New York. The city on Lake Erie was developing rapidly at the time: the economy was growing and cultural life was flourishing. In 1881 it hosted the ninth congress of the Association for the Advancement of Women with 975 women and 25 men. It was there that Bethune announced that she was opening her own architectural firm, thus becoming the first independent woman architect in the United States. She ran her office with her husband and partner, and together they built many industrial and commercial buildings as well as eighteen school buildings. Her authorship is particularly well documented for the Hotel Lafayette in Buffalo, whose rooms featured hot and cold running water and a telephone, which were very advanced at the time.[16] The Western Association of Architects decided in 1885: "if the lady is practicing architecture and is in good standing, there is no reason why she should not be one of us." In 1888, Louise Blanchard Bethune was elected the first female member of the American Institute of Architects (AIA), which marked the beginning of her commitment to the politics of the profession. She rejected special regard as a woman in this profession: "there is no need whatever of a woman architect…. The woman architect has exactly the same work to do as a man. When a woman enters the profession she will be met kindly and will be welcome but not as a woman, only as an architect."[17]

Signe Hornborg (1862–1926): The First Academic Degree

Finland was the first European country to grant women access to architectural studies. From 1870 onward, women could be granted special permission to study at its universities. In 1888, Signe Hornborg graduated from the Polytechnic Institute in Helsinki, which had been founded by Czar Nicholas I, as Grand Duke of Finland, in 1849. In 1890, she was granted special permission to take the final exam. Shortly thereafter, she designed, for no fee, a new fire station in Porvoo, near Helsinki.[18] She then worked in the office of Elias Heikel and later for Lars Sonck, one of the most famous proponents of Art Nouveau in Finland. Her first significant project of her own was a residence she designed in 1892, the "Signellina"—named after her—in Pori in southwestern Finland. Five years later, she was allowed to design the facade of a large apartment building in Helsinki, but as a woman she was excluded from the overall planning of the building.

Marion Mahony Griffin (1871–1961): In the Shadow of Two Architects

At the age of twenty-three, the young architect Marion Mahony received her degree from the Massachusetts Institute of Technology (MIT) in 1894 with a thesis titled "The House and Studios of a Painter" and became the first woman architect in the United States with a state license to practice the profession. In 1895, she was the first female employee in Frank Lloyd Wright's office in Chicago. He called her a "gifted assistant."[19] Mahony's great talent as a draftswoman in the Beaux Arts style, which is characterized by horizontal lines, deep eaves, and geometric ornament, made her almost indispensable for Wright in the years that followed. Her drawings became the public trademarks of Frank Lloyd Wright's plans, and her style would later be employed by many other architects of Chicago's Prairie School. She herself took over increasing responsibility in Wright's studio and developed a friendly connection to the Wright family.

The irreconcilable break between them came when Frank Lloyd Wright left his office and family in Chicago behind in 1909 and traveled through Europe with the wife of a client. When he was preparing his first large monograph for the Wasmuth Verlag in Berlin in 1910, Mahony's drawings were used as the basis for the lithographs, but the monogram with which she always

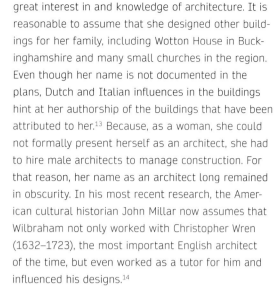

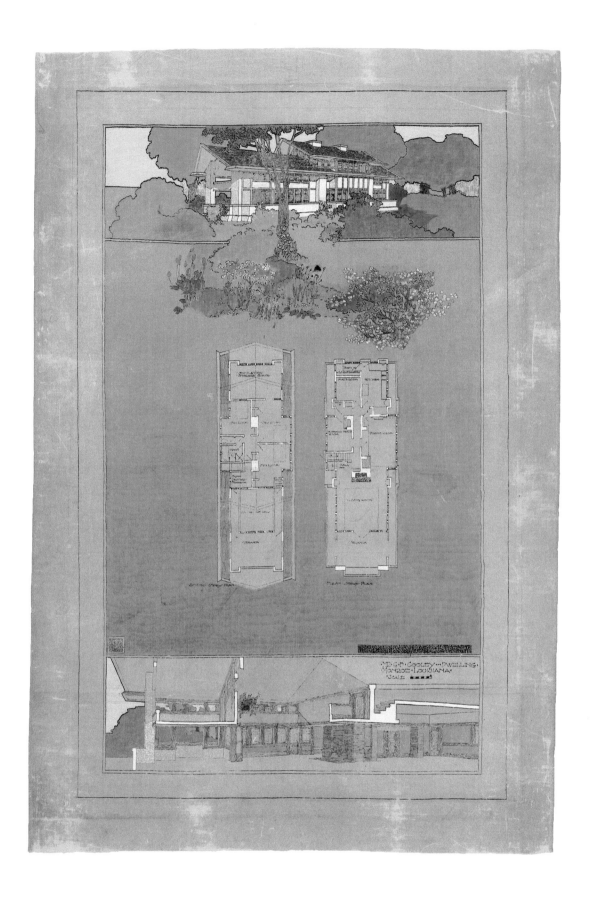

Marion Mahony Griffin, plan for the G. B. Cooley House in Monroe, Louisiana, 1910, watercolor on silk, 110 × 75 cm. The Cooley House was not built until 1920 and is one of the last remaining Prairie-style buildings in the US. The monogram of Marion Mahony Griffin is located in the lower left corner of the floor plans.

Marion Mahony Griffin

Julia Morgan

signed her drawings was removed. Wright might have seen her beautiful, linear, floral drawing style with a Japanese inflection as serious competition for the design of his buildings. Wright never publicly gave credit in his lifetime to his most important employee, neither for her drawings nor for her contribution to his designs.[20] During his absence, Marion Mahony handled the studio's ongoing projects. Another of the employees was Walter Burley Griffin, six years her junior, whom she married in 1911. She encouraged him to enter a highly publicized competition for Canberra, which had just been designated Australia's new capital, and supported him by working on his design. He won the competition, but there are some who attribute the first prize to Marion Mahony Griffin's impressive, 1.7-meter-wide perspectives in sepia and natural tones and the black-and-white ink drawings on canvas. The project was never built.

Marion Mahony Griffin was never concerned about her own reputation or authorship; for her, collaboration with her husband was more important, and that applied to subsequent projects in India as well. When she returned to Chicago after his death in 1937, she made the preservation and dissemination of his architectural work her life's task. This resulted in the four-volume publication *The Magic of America*,[21] an homage to her late husband, memories and an assessment of Frank Lloyd Wright, and an account of her own philosophy of life, based on the values of integrity, democracy, and the verity of the artistic statement.

Julia Morgan (1872–1957): An Unprecedented Career

Only on her second attempt was Julia Morgan accepted to study architecture at the most respected architecture school in Europe: the École des Beaux-Arts in Paris. In 1896, she was rejected as a woman, but then she was admitted two years later. Because women were only allowed to study up to the age of thirty, Morgan took her exams after only three years and returned to her native United States with her diploma in 1902. Julia Morgan made a conscious decision to live independently without a family in order to devote herself completely to her profession.

In 1904, she was the first woman to be granted an architect's license in California and began an unprecedented career by founding her own studio in San Francisco: more than 700 buildings are documented as her work.[22]

Julia Morgan designed schools, churches, hospitals, and many commercial and residential buildings. She had a masterly understanding of European historicism, which she had studied in Paris and employed it in playful ways, above all in her stately buildings for the major American publisher William Randolph Hearst. For more than twenty-five years, she worked for Hearst and had a unusually respectful client-architect relationship, designing, among other things, his artificial castle: Hearst Castle. Her great passion was designing a magnificent swimming hall, which

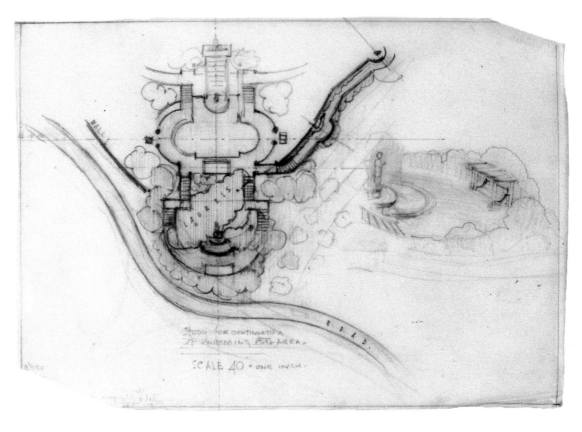

Julia Morgan, Hearst Castle, study for the extension of the Neptune Pool complex, original drawing

Julia Morgan, Hearst Castle, San Simeon, CA, 1919–37. The property was planned and built as an enormous vacation home intended to house the extensive art collection of media mogul William Randolph Hearst. With structural extensions and additions of original spolia from Europe, the complex was created as a fantasy castle with an eclectic architecture inspired by European styles.

Julia Morgan and William Randolph Hearst, 1926, on the construction site of Hearst Castle

The Roman Bath at Hearst Castle. The walls, ceilings, and floors of the swimming pool are decorated with a mosaic of blue and gold Murano tiles.

was modeled on a Roman bath. She also designed for Hearst an ensemble of Gothic stone and half-timber houses in the mountains of California that was supposed to recall a "Bavarian village" of the Old World.

Morgan was also active in women's organizations. For example, in 1934 she designed a clubhouse for the Monday Club in San Luis Obispo, for which she combined a Mediterranean aesthetic with elements from the Arts and Crafts movement. In lieu of a fee, she asked for room and board whenever she attended the Monday Club. She also supported the Young Women's Christian Association (YWCA), a social organization for which she designed several buildings in California, commissioned by Phoebe Apperson Hearst, William Randolph Hearst's mother. After World War II, her architecture was no longer in demand, and she was not interested in the popular modernist style of architecture. After Hearst died in 1951, she retired from the profession at the age of seventy-nine and had most of her drawings and documents burned, so few survive.

Julia Morgan never left behind a list of her works nor spoke publicly or wrote about her work during her career. Not until the nineteen-seventies did the architectural historian Sarah Holmes Boutelle

begin searching for her buildings. Among other things, she was able to document the spectacular commission for Hearst Castle in California. It therefore took nearly a century for her work as an architect to be reported publicly at all.[23] It was only in 2014 that Julia Morgan was posthumously awarded the gold medal of the American Institute of Architects (AIA). It was the first time this important award was given to a woman architect.

Elisabeth von Knobelsdorff (1877–1959): Working in the Civil Service

After women began to be admitted to German universities in 1909, it became possible to train as an architect, but professional independence continued to be more difficult, because women were forced into domestic work or their competence was questioned.[24] It is therefore astonishing that the architect Elisabeth von Knobelsdorff managed to secure a position in the civil service.

The von Knobelsdorff family was from Silesia and lived on Jakobsdorf manor near Breslau (now Wrocław). In 1915, four years after passing her exam and receiving her engineering degrees from

19

[KENNWORT. SCHLESISCHE ART]

Elisabeth von Knobelsdorff,
community center for a Silesian estate,
original drawing

the Königlich Technische Hochschule (Royal Technical College) in Charlottenburg, she planned and built a community house for the village that continued to be used as a social center until 1946. She was called up during World War I as a field architect with the rank of lieutenant and designed the so-called Knobelsdorff-Baracken (barracks) and a military hospital on the Döberitz military training grounds west of Berlin.[25] After World War I ended, the higher civil service career path was opened to women on an equal basis: Elisabeth von Knobelsdorff passed the required exam in 1921 and was the first architect to be granted the (male) title *Regierungsbaumeister* (government architect). As part of reductions to the civil service in the nineteen-twenties, which affected primarily married women, she was dismissed from public service as a "second salary earner." She continued to work in Berlin as a freelance architect until she and her husband moved to Boston in 1927.[26] After he was called back to Berlin in 1938, she was unable to resume her professional activity under the National Socialist regime, which preferred to see women in the kitchen and not in higher professions.

Margarete Schütte-Lihotzky (1897–2000): Building for Women

In 1919, Margarete Lihotzky was the first woman to complete studies at the Kunstgewerbeschule (School

of the Applied Arts) in Vienna, where architects such as Josef Hoffmann and Heinrich Tessenow were teaching at the time. That same year, she accompanied Viennese school children from her drawing class on a trip to Rotterdam. In her free time, she closely studied the city's progressive housing complexes and attended lectures by Hendrik Petrus Berlage, the father of modern architecture in the Netherlands. The experiences of that trip would crucially influence her sociopolitical stance as an architect.[27]

After she returned to Vienna, she worked for one of the city's large housing construction companies alongside Adolf Loos and Richard Neutra. In 1926, municipal architect Ernst May hired her for the Hochbauamt (Building Office) of the City of Frankfurt am Main, where she took a position in the standardization department to study rationalization and economy in the implementation of standardized housing. Her most famous contribution was the famous Frankfurter Küche (Frankfurt Kitchen), which was intended to simplify the work of housewives. This type of kitchen featured a long, narrow floor plan with built-in elements and equipment designed precisely to suit the movements of kitchen work.[28] Kitchens of this type were installed in around 10,000 apartments in the housing developments of Neues Frankfurt (New Frankfurt), which was being built at that time. In 1927, she married her colleague Wilhelm Schütte and lost her job because of the new law prohibiting

Elisabeth von Knobelsdorf

Margarete Schütte-Lihotzky

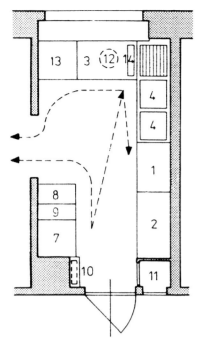

Smallest apartment of the "Zwofa" type (two-family house), which Schütte-Lihotzky developed in 1928 for the Frankfurt building construction office. The wall furniture she developed enables the room to have two functions: during the day, a table and chairs are placed in the middle of the room; at night, they are pushed aside and beds roll out to transform the main room into a bedroom.

Top
Margarete Schütte-Lihotzky, floor plan of the Frankfurt kitchen. The arrangement of fixtures, appliances, and passageways is designed according to the precise movements of the housewife.

Top right
Margarete Schütte-Lihotzky, Frankfurt kitchen, original version from the nineteen-twenties, which is exhibited in the permanent collection of the Werkbundarchiv – Museum der Dinge. This type of kitchen represented a significant step in the rationalization of household management and modernization of the living environment. It became the prototype of the modern fitted kitchen.

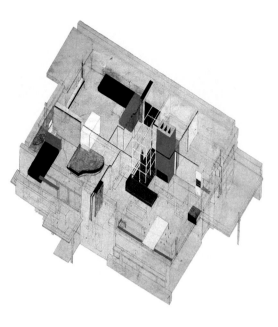

Truus Schröder, Rietveldt Schröder
House, Utrecht, 1923. With the use
of primary colors, geometric shapes,
and an open floor plan, the house
is a perfect expression of De Stjil.

Axonometric drawing after completion
of construction for the color scheme and
equipment of the upper floor

Truus Schröder

The open floor plan enabled Schröder to realize her idea of a variable living space for the whole family.

married couples from earning two salaries in public service; her husband remained in his position.

In the following years, Schütte-Lihotzky was repeatedly commissioned by Frankfurt's Hochbauamt for architectural tasks, including kindergartens and housing types designed to meet the needs of underprivileged social groups, such as the *Musterwohnung für die alleinstehende berufstätige Frau* (Model Apartment for the Working Single Woman) project of 1928.[29]

When Ernst May was invited to Moscow in 1930 to take over the planning of housing construction in Soviet cities of heavy industry, Schütte-Lihotzky and her husband followed him. She was assigned the department for children's facilities until she had to leave the country in 1937. In the fitful years shortly before the outbreak of World War II, the Schüttes traveled through Europe and ultimately ended up in Istanbul, where Margarete Schütte-Lihotzky joined the Communist Party and worked to combat the National Socialist regime, which during a stay in Vienna in 1940 led to her arrest and lengthy imprisonment. When the war ended, her communist past made it difficult for her to return to her profession. Internationally, however, she continued to be in demand as an expert and consultant on architecture for apartments and kindergartens. After she died in 2000, a street in Frankfurt am Main was to be renamed after her, but conservative politicians successfully blocked the initiative using the argument that she had been a Stalinist.

Truus Schröder (1889–1985): Like-Minded Client and Partner

Through her contact with the De Stijl artists' group, Truus Schröder, a young mother, developed clear ideas about the education of her children, an independent life as a single mother, and modernist ideas for housing.

She completed her training as a pharmacist and, at the age of twenty-two, married the lawyer Frits Schröder, who was eleven years older, and had three children with him. She first met her future life partner, Gerrit Rietveld, an architect and a member of De Stijl, in 1921 when Schröder hired him to redesign a room in her home to suit her reformist cultural ideas. Their architectural collaboration, which would lead to a lifelong friendship and love, began in 1923 with the design for a residence in Utrecht that Truus Schröder wanted to build for herself and her three children after the death of her husband. The house was intended to be the perfect expression of De Stijl:

primary colors, geometrical forms, and an unconventional open floor plan.

She wanted to see all of its ideas realized in the house Rietveld was to design for her: a simple geometric form with large windows, a variable design for the interior with sliding doors and fluid transitions from interior to exterior. On the upper story was a large, open space where parents and children could have conversations: a room in which the family could live, work, and sleep, and whose size was adjustable thanks to the sliding elements.

In a letter, Rietveld wrote her: "You have showered the world with ideas: people say I am a man of many ideas, but you have many more. I sweep them together around you. And they are not some old ideas; they have a new orientation. facilities … We have to continue working together as a team."[30]

Rietveld, who was in fact trained as a carpenter, opened his architectural firm after building Schröder's house, and until 1933 he ran it from there—in close interchange with her professionally. In the nineteen-thirties, they worked together on a project for four row houses with model furnishings and planned the conversion of a large residential building in Haarlem into one-room apartments for single working women.[31] Only after the death of his wife did Rietveld move into the house, where he lived with Truus Schröder until he died.

Schröder also addressed the theories of new forms of social housing. In the feminist journal edited by her sister, *De Werkende Vrouw: In Huis en Maatschappij* (The Working Woman: At Home and in Society), she wrote an article about the Frankfurt kitchen and the social importance of good interior architecture.[32] Although their contemporaries mentioned her participation in Gerrit Rietveld's design of her house many times, her architectural contribution was later ignored completely. Without Truus Schröder, what is now called the Rietveld-Schröder House would surely not have become the icon of architectural history that it is today.[33]

Hilde Reiss (1909–2002): Bauhaus Graduate and Pioneer of the Case Study House

Reiss came to the Bauhaus in 1929 and from 1930 studied architecture in Dessau under the directorship of Hannes Meyer until she received her diploma in 1932.[34] She was thus one of only four women who received a diploma in the field of architecture during

Hilde Reiss, Idea House II, 1947, street-
side facade. With this precursor of the
Case Study House, she and participating
architects William Friedman and Malcolm
Lein sought to familiarize the public with
good architecture and design.

Floor plans, upper floor and basement.
The split-level house with open floor
plan is designed for a family with two
children. The private rooms could
be separated from the flowing space
by means of folding partitions.

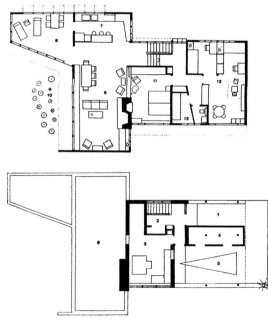

Hilde Reiss

the entire existence of the Bauhaus. In practice, the equal rights of man and woman proclaimed in the beginning of the Bauhaus remained a myth at the historical institution. Walter Gropius, the first director of the Bauhaus, was already calling for the reduction of the percentage of women by increasing tuition and shunting female students into the less highly regarded arts of weaving and pottery after they completed the preliminary course. Participation in the unofficial architecture course that he offered at his firm was reserved exclusively for men.[35] Only after the architect Hannes Meyer was appointed to the Bauhaus in 1928 was the architecture department "formalized," and women—including Hilde Reiss—allowed to take part in its courses.

Because she was being pursued for printing anti-Nazi leaflets, she fled to New York in 1933, where she found a position in the office of the famous designer Gilbert Rohde and taught with him at the Design Laboratory, a modernist art school. Together with the architect William Friedman, Reiss went to work as a curator at the Walker Art Center in Minneapolis in 1945, the first museum in the United States to establish a permanent exhibition of modern architecture and design. She edited the museum's journal, *Every Day Quarterly: A Guide to Well Designed Products*, in which she addressed questions of modern housing and good design.

At the Walker Art Center, she was able to continue and refine the Bauhaus idea of a totalizing design that comprised the arts of painting, sculpture, and architecture as a pedagogical experiment. Together with William Friedman, she developed the precursor of the Case Study House, for which there was already a specific housing type in Idea House I of 1941. Idea House II was supposed to provide the public with a model of good architecture and design. Reiss adopted the principles of modern design for the spaces. Together with Friedman, she developed an open floor plan for a family with two children, which thanks to flexible partition walls permitted all their activities: eating, play, work, and entertainment. Idea House II was built on the museum grounds in 1947 and offered its accommodations temporarily to a variety of guests, including a family of four, a trio of working women, and a newlywed couple. It was a precursor to the Case Study Houses that were later built in the United States and attracted a great deal of attention throughout the country.

Lilly Reich (1885–1947): Master at the Bauhaus

At the Bauhaus, women often stood in the shadows of their male masters. One of those who was able to step out of those shadows was Lilly Reich. Thanks to her collaboration and personal relationship with Ludwig Mies van der Rohe, the interior and textile designer was appointed master in the architecture/furnishing department at the Bauhaus in Dessau under his directorship in 1932.

Lilly Reich, Café Samt & Seide, *Die Mode der Dame,* Berlin, 1927. Mies and Reich developed the exhibition stand for the German silk industry as a flowing space, which was structured exclusively through silk fabric panels. The product to be presented was thus also a central element of the exhibition design. The stand was used as a café and furnished with the recently developed cantilever chairs and tubular steel tables.

Weissenhof Chair, designed by Lilly Reich

Tugendhat House, 1929–30, Brno, Czech Republic. A semi-circular partition separates the dining area from the 237-square-meter open plan living room and transforms it into an intimate dining niche. The design of the house and interior is the result of collaboration between Ludwig Mies van der Rohe and Lilly Reich.

Lilly Reich was born in Berlin and began an apprenticeship as a machine embroiderer in 1905. She thus recognized early on the advantages of combining craft and machine production. She was able to employ that experience as early as 1908 at the Wiener Werkstätte für Kunsthandwerk (Viennese Workshop for Crafts), and she would take advantage of it all her life. After returning to Berlin, she became a member of the Deutscher Werkbund and opened a studio for interior design. There she created her first designs for furniture and interior furnishings. In 1926, she moved her studio to Frankfurt am Main and that same year met Mies van der Rohe. One year later, she returned to Berlin. There she began an intense collaboration with Mies van der Rohe on the Werkbund exhibition *Die Wohnung* (The Home) in Stuttgart. Based on their great success in Stuttgart, the two were commissioned to be artistic directors of the German contribution to the World's Fair in Barcelona in 1928, for which Mies van der Rohe designed the legendary pavilion for the German Reich. At that time, he also began to design the Tugendhat House in Brno, Czechoslovakia, which would, like the German Pavilion in Barcelona, become an icon in the history of architecture. The interior design of the Tugendhat House was also a close collaboration of "Reich and Mies," as their colleagues called them. After Reich was dismissed from the Bauhaus when the institution was closed down, and Mies van der Rohe went into exile in Chicago, Lilly Reich continued to work as an interior architect in Berlin. Her participation in large industrial exhibitions in Berlin and Paris in 1937 certainly placed her in the service of National Socialist propaganda. After the war, she took up teaching again at the Hochschule für Bildende Künste in Berlin, but she had to resign her position in 1946 for health reasons. Lilly Reich died in Berlin in 1947.

Lilly Reich's involvement in Ludwig Mies van der Rohe's design is still not adequately appreciated, even though the signature of his designs was clearly altered from the beginning of their collaboration. His interest in furniture design was also first manifested after meeting Reich; nevertheless, people continue to speak of "Mies van der Rohe chairs" to this day.

Lilly Reich

Even today, women architects all over the world still struggle for recognition. The personal positions that follow are dedicated to four great women architects: Emilie Winkelmann (p. 29), Eileen Gray (p. 35), Lina Bo Bardi (p. 43), and Zaha Hadid (p. 49).
The important contribution made by contemporary women architects to the global culture of architecture is impressively documented in the second part of this publication with thirty-six projects by women, all of whom have presented their work in the series "Architecture Today—Women in Architecture" at the Universität Tübingen.

1   The selection was made with intention of presenting different personalities who, under different conditions and in their own specific ways, managed to assert themselves in the male-dominated world of architecture.

2   Marcus Vitruvius Pollio, *De architectura libri decem*, presumably Rome, ca. 25 BC.

3   Leon Battista Alberti, *De re aedificatoria* (Florence, 1452).

4   Andrea Palladio, *I quattro libri dell'architettura* (Venice, 1570).

5   See Ilaria Hoppe, "Plautilla Bricci, die erste Architektin: Zum Verhältnis von Architektur und Geschlecht im römischen Seicento," in *Frauen und Päpste: Zur Konstruktion von Weiblichkeit in Kunst und Urbanistik des römischen Seicento*, ed. Eckhard Leuschner and Iris Wenderholm (Berlin, 2016), pp. 179–82.

6   Dietrich Erben, "Architektur als öffentliche Angelegenheit: Ein berufssoziologisches Porträt des Architekten im Barock," in *Der Architekt: Geschichte und Gegenwart eines Berufsstandes*, ed. Winfried Nerdinger, exh. cat. Pinakothek der Moderne (Munich, 2012), p. 112.

7   See "Geschichte der Frauen an der ETH," in *ETH Zürich*, www.ethz.ch/services/de/anstellung-und-arbeit/arbeitsumfeld/chancengleichheit/strategie-und-zahlen/frauen-an-der-eth/geschichte-der-frauen-an-der-eth.html (accessed August 28, 2020).

8   The first documented female architecture student at the Polytechnikum (now ETH) in Zurich was an American woman in 1900. In 1923, the first woman received an architecture diploma. See the exhibition texts of the *Frau Architekt* at the Zentrum Architektur in Zurich, February 28–May 10, 2020, www.zaz-bellerive.ch/wp-content/uploads/2020/06/015_011901_Frau_Architekt_Saaltext-Journal_DE_RZ_200225_HR.pdf (accessed August 28, 2020).

9   See Consuelo Lollobrigida, *Plautilla Bricci: Pictura et Architectura Celebris; L'architettrice del Barocco Romano* (Rome, 2018).

10   A substantial notebook from 1656 on the construction of the Villa Benedetti outside of the Porta San Pancrazio, which documents the architect's planning and management of the building, is found in the Archivio di Stato, Rome. In a contract dated October 15, 1663, the client, Benedetti, agrees to pay the architect, Marco Antonio Beragiola, to complete everything according to the plans by "signora Plautilla Briccia architecttrice." See Lollobrigida 2018 (see note 9), fig. 40.

11   Matteo Mayer, *La Villa Benedetta Decritta* (Rome, 1667). In the engraving, one is struck by the fact that the street facade was built on a base of artificial rock, which is the only part that survived the destruction of the villa during the war of independence in 1849, which clearly documents a later change in plan. Bernini adopted this very motif in the design for his unrealized proposal for a new building for the Louvre in Paris. It was probably at his suggestion that the idea of the rock base was adopted by the architect for the Benedetti Villa in Rome. See Hoppe 2016 (see note 5), p. 177.

12   Lynne Walker, ed., *Drawing and Diversity: Women, Architecture and Practice*, exh. cat., RIBA Heinz Gallery (London, 1996).

13   John Millar, "The first woman architect," in: *The Architects' Journal* online, 11.11.2010, www.architectsjournal.co.uk/practice/culture/the-first-woman-architect (accessed August 28, 2020).

14   Millar's attribution of more than 400 buildings to her is controversial; the publication on them that was announced for 2012 has not yet appeared.

15   See Adriana Barbasch, "Louise Blanchard Bethune," in *Architecture: A Place for Women*, ed. Ellen Perry Berkeley (Washington, DC, 1989), pp. 15–25.

16   Ibid., p. 20.

17   From a speech by Louis Blanchard Bethune in 1881, quoted in ibid., p. 24.

18   See "#architetta Signe Hornborg / Finland.The Unforgettables," Facebook post by Rebelarchitette, May 8, 2018, www.facebook.com/architettearchiwomen/posts/architetta-signe-hornborg-finlandthe-unforgettablessigne-ida-katarina-hornborg-1/2060054694008829/ (accessed August 29, 2020).

19   On her life, see Elizabeth Joy Birmingham, "Marion Mahony Griffin and The Magic of America: Recovery, Reaction and Re-Entrenchment in the Discourse of Architectural Studies," PhD diss., Iowa State University, 2000, lib.dr.iastate.edu/rtd/12310 (accessed August 29, 2020).

20   I am grateful to Anthony Alofsin for this reference. See also Anthony Alofsin, *Frank Lloyd Wright: The Lost Years, 1910–1922* (Chicago, 1993).

21   Marion Mahony Griffin, *The Magic of America*, 1894, electronic edition (Chicago, 2007). archive.artic.edu/magicofamerica/ (accessed August 29, 2020).

22   See Sarah Holmes Boutelle, "An Elusive Pioneer: Tracing the Work of Julia Morgan," in *Architecture: A Place for Women*, ed. Ellen Perry Berkeley (Washington, DC, 1989) and Sarah Holmes Boutelle, *Julia Morgan, Architect* (New York, 1988).

23   Ibid.

24   Patricia Mazón, "Das akademische Bürgerrecht und die Zulassung von Frauen zu den deutschen Universitäten, 1865–1914," in: *Akademisches Bürgerrecht und Frauenstudium*, www.gender.hu-berlin.de/de/publikationen/gender-bulletin-broschueren/bulletin-texte/texte-23/texte23pkt2.pdf/at_download/file (accessed August 29, 2020).

25   Helga Schmidt-Thomsen, "Frauen in der Architektur: Neue Berufswege seit der Jahrhundertwende," in *Architektinnenhistorie: Zur Geschichte der Architektinnen und Designerinnen im 20. Jahrhundert, eine erste Zusammenstellung; Katalog zu einer Ausstellung vom 11.–30.10.1984 anlässlich. des 7. Internationalen Kongresses der Architektinnen, Städteplanerinnen und Landschaftsplanerinnen* in Berlin, ed. International Union of Women Architects, Bauausstellung (West Berlin, 1987), p. 24.

26   See Kerstin Dörhöfer, *Pionierinnen in der Architektur: Eine Baugeschichte der Moderne* (Tübingen, 2004), pp. 38–43.

27   Sonia Ricon Baldessarini, *Wie Frauen bauen: Architektinnen von Julia Morgan bis Zaha Hadid* (Berlin, 2001), pp. 64–80.

28   An original kitchen has been preserved in the Museum Angewandte Kunst in Frankfurt am Main since November 2017, and is part of the permanent collection. I am grateful to the responsible curator, Dr. Christos-Nikolas Vittoratos, for pointing out that the Frankfurt kitchen was a collaborative work, produced with the essential participation of the kitchen engineers Anni and Otto Haarer. See also Christina Treutlein, "Die Aluminium-Schütten in der Frankfurter Küche," *ernst-maygesellschaft e.v.*, July 2019, www.ernst-may-gesellschaft.de/einzelnachricht-home/exponat-des-monats-juli-2019.html (accessed August 31, 2020).

29   Stella Rollig, "Für die alleinstehende berufstätige Frau: Die soziale Architektur der Margarete Schütte-Lihotzky; Eine Ausstellung im Wiener MAK," *taz*, June 23, 1993, www.taz.de/!1918622/ (accessed August 31, 2020).

30   Quoted in Dörte Kuhlmann, *Raum, Macht & Differenz: Genderstudien in der Architektur* (Vienna, 2005), p. 28.

31   Alice T. Friedman, *Women and the Making of the Modern House: A Social and Architectural History* (New York, 1998), p. 88.

32   Ibid., p. 80.

33   The Rietveld-Schröder House was declared a "Rijksmonument," a historical landmark, in 1976 and has also been on the list of UNESCO World Heritage Sites since 2000. See "Rietveld-Schröder-Haus," de.wikipedia.org/wiki/Rietveld-Schr%C3%B6der-Haus (accessed August 22, 2020).

34   Inge Schaefer Horton, *Early Women Architects of the San Francisco Bay Area: The Lives and Work of Fifty Professionals, 1890–1951* (Jefferson, NC, 2010), p. 353.

35   Gropius wrote in a letter in 1921: "According to our experiences, it is not advisable for women to work in the heavy craft operations such as carpentry, etc. … We therefore speak out on principle against the training women as architects." Quoted in Ulrike Müller, *Bauhaus Frauen. Meisterinnen in Kunst, Handwerk und Design* (Munich, 2019), p. 104. Translated by Steven Lindberg.

Festsaalbau

Emilie Winkelmann

The First Academically Trained Female Architect in Germany

Dirk Boll

Emilie Winkelmann

Theater Blumenstrasse in Berlin, 1907.
The architect won the competition for a
theater building in the first year of her
professional life.

Emilie Winkelmann cannot be omitted from a portrayal of women in architecture. According to her own statement, she considered herself the first woman "to have studied architecture and to have independently carried out the architectural profession, project planning, and overall management of buildings." As she affirmed: "Before me, no woman, not even a foreigner, has studied architecture." Even though it probably escaped her notice that at the same time, and even somewhat earlier, other women had acquired the subject academically and conquered it successfully as a field of activity, this does not diminish her status as an important pioneer in the field of women's emancipation. In contrast to Winkelmann, I am neither an architect nor an architectural historian and am therefore not in a position to adequately acknowledge her significance in architectural history. Nevertheless, she is close to me, as a special personality, as an intelligent networker, but above all as the creator of a building in which I have lived for several years.

Emilie Winkelmann was born on May 8, 1875, in Aken, Anhalt. Her grandfather ran a carpentry business with an associated building contractor. Here she completed an apprenticeship and acquired basic construction knowledge, especially in the field of timber construction. However, the next logical step, the study of architecture, was not open to her; women were not admitted to scientific universities in the Kingdom of Prussia until 1909. Instead, she enrolled in the summer semester of 1902 at the Technische Hochschule Hannover for the "Studium Generale" with a focus on technology, but according to the regulations, only as an auditor. However, she did succeed in obtaining "exceptional admission" as a guest student at the faculty of architecture, where she completed a regular course of study in architecture from the winter semester 1902/03 onward. She had signed the underlying application "E. Winkelmann," which might have been interpreted as "Emil Winkelmann." However, in 1906 she was refused admission to the exams because she was a woman. She left the university,

moved to prosperous Berlin, found employment in a planning office, and became self-employed the following year. She was not allowed to call herself an engineering graduate because she lacked an academic degree, but the professional title of architect was not yet protected at that time.

Building a Career in Imperial Germany

While her office was still in its first year, Winkelmann won first prize in a competition for a hall with several festival rooms in Blumenstrasse in Berlin. In contrast to her competitors, she solved the task of designing the development in such a way that the visitors got in each other's way as little as possible when events were taking place simultaneously—and was awarded the contract for her project. The following year, this project attracted attention in the publication *Angewandte Kunst*. Under the pseudonym Jarno Jessen, the art writer Anna Michaelson selected and depicted the Blumenstrasse hall building along with three designs from 1903 and 1907, but concealed the architect's academic training: "Emilie Winkelmann received her training as an architect in Berlin studios." After the Ottoman Empire entered World War I as an ally of the German Empire, Winkelmann was commissioned by the Oriental Institute of Berlin University to do the preparatory work for what was then Germany's most prominent project abroad, the Haus der Freundschaft in Constantinople. Among the participants in the 1916 competition were Peter Behrens, Paul Bonatz, Hugo Eberhardt, Martin Elsässer, August Endell, Theodor Fischer, Bruno Paul, Hans Poelzig, Richard Riemerschmid, Bruno Taut, and, as the winner of the competition, German Bestelmeyer. She herself had not been invited to enter the competition. The course of the war prevented the project from continuing after the laying of the foundation stone. From the very beginning, the architect's work was characterized by a wide range of building types, with residential buildings, theater and exhibition buildings, functional

agricultural buildings, and production facilities. In the 1912 exhibition *Die Frau in Haus und Beruf* in Berlin, Winkelmann showed twenty-six of her own designs. Her growing office reflected this early success; at times she had as many as fifteen employees. In 1928 she was admitted to the Association of German Architects (BDA).

The Leistikowhaus

In addition to public commissions with popular appeal, Winkelmann realized a whole series of residential buildings in the years before and after World War I. One of the biggest contracts awarded to her at the beginning of her career as a freelance architect was the construction of an apartment building for a wealthy, upper middle-class clientele just outside Berlin. Between 1866 and the turn of the century, an elegant residential quarter was established in the west of the then still independent city of Charlottenburg, known as Westend after the example of London. Benefiting from its early development as a district for country houses with large garden plots and the opening of the Ringbahn in 1877, Westend quickly became Charlottenburg's preferred residential area. On the border with Grunewald, Neu-Westend was built on the southern edge of this villa district from 1906 onward with spacious apartment buildings. In the street named after the painter Walter Leistikow, Winkelmann planned and built a large apartment building from 1909 to 1910, which she later named the Leistikowhaus. The client's decision to entrust the young

architect with such a large and important project indicates the prestige she had already acquired shortly after founding her office. Her ability to plan and execute such a building within two years speaks for her skill at networking within the craftsmen's and suppliers' circles.

There are four apartments per floor, organized around two atriums. The main staircase has an elevator (then a technological innovation), and all apartments also have service entrances and the corresponding utility staircases. The apartments are generously dimensioned. The smaller ones at the back cover about 190 square meters, while the ones at the front are one half again as large. What they all have in common is their luxurious furnishing, with paneling, stuccowork, double glazing, and painted black-figure ornamental windows to the inner courtyards. In addition, the house was provided with a marble-clad entrance hall.

Since then, the building has had an eventful past. The records tell of applications for the installation of additional stoves during the cold wartime winters, its use by the British occupying forces as an "officers' residence" from 1945 to 1952, and a party cellar, which unfortunately has not been preserved. In 1963, the first floor was converted into a hotel, which in 1965 expanded onto the second floor as well. Presumably the wall, which we, as inhabitants of one of the apartments, removed in 2015, had been installed to separate one of the twelve guest rooms. When the building was transferred to floor ownership in 1979, some of the apartments were divided. From 2014

Leistikowhaus, 1910, Berlin. The apartment building in Neu-Westend with luxurious furnishings and a modern elevator was completed in only two years.

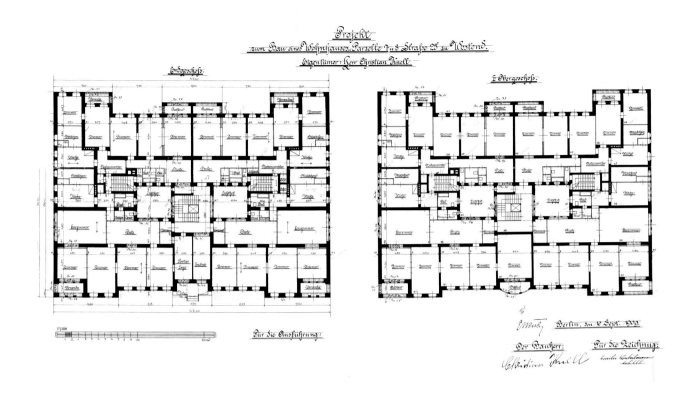

Leistikowhaus, floor plan. As a free-standing building, the plan does not follow the classic Berlin perimeter block development. Winkelmann's arrangement allows four spacious, light-filled apartments per floor.

onward, we have tried to reverse such interventions and restore the apartment's original proportions.

Several distinctive features set the Leistikowhaus apart from the average apartment block. Since the building is not integrated into a perimeter block—rather, it is a freestanding structure—the foor plan does not have to follow the usual Berlin disposition, in which two or three salons in the front building facing the street are connected to a number of rooms in the side wing via a large, usually poorly lit space known as a "Berlin Room." Instead, the apartments are grouped around a large "hallway" that serves as a central access point. With the exception of the dining rooms, the main rooms are located on the long sides of the building, and the dining rooms and the ancillary rooms on the two narrow sides. Visitors are subtly guided: the doors through which they are intended to pass are extra-high, glazed double doors, while private passages are correspondingly lower, narrower, and with closed door leaves. Situated parallel to the hallway, the main rooms on the two long sides of the house form two classic enfilades of rooms that flow into each other, the main axes of which measure twenty-three and nearly eighteen meters, respectively, at the front. One does not live in two or three front representation rooms and countless rear chambers lined up along a narrow corridor in the traditional Berlin manner, but in a sequence of equally large and well-proportioned rooms. The wall-mounted furnishings have been almost completely preserved, and the restrained, modern design of the woodwork and cast brass reveal the architect's high quality standards.

The stained glass by Gottfried Heinersdorff comes from the famous Berlin Kunstanstalt für Glasmalerei, Bleiverglasung und Glasmosaik. The designs have been preserved in the archives of the Berlinische Galerie. Like the other five buildings by Winkelmann in Berlin that survived the war, the Leistikowhaus is now a listed building.

Winkelmann's Networks

Emilie Winkelmann's success was based on her skills as an architect, but also on her talent for using networks to acquire customers. Even in her early years, a successfully completed contract opened up new circles for her: it is said that two male colleagues had already failed in the renovation of the Pension Tscheuschner in Berlin. Winkelmann revised the floor plans and relocated the entrance, which enabled a significant improvement in use. Apparently, the Tscheuschner was frequented by the Prussian landed gentry, which provided the architect with a large number of follow-up orders. Advertisement by word-of-mouth proved to be so effective that building contracts in rural areas, from the reconstruction of castles to agricultural and forestry buildings, secured work for the office for more than thirty years. Its aristocratic clientele also saved her during World War II. As the bombing of Berlin intensified, Winkelmann was able to stay with one of her clients, the von der Schulenburg family, at Gut Hovedissen near Bielefeld. She died there in 1951, after having been actively involved in planning the postwar reconstruction.

Leistikowhaus, apartment on the second floor. When the apartment was restored in 2014, it was returned to its original proportions. The enfilade of light-flooded main rooms is is situated on the long side of the building.

More interesting for Winkelmann than the rural nobility of the late German Empire, however, was her
participation in a metropolitan network of influential
women, which also included the wealthy entrepre-
neur's widow and women's rights activist Ottilie von
Hansemann. In 1908, von Hansemann offered the
rector of the Friedrich-Wilhelms-Universität in Berlin
a foundation for the benefit of female students, who
were by now generally admitted in all countries of
the Empire except Prussia. There, the lecturers could
continue to deny women participation in their courses,
which was a regular occurrence. However, since the
minister of culture was not prepared to put a stop to
this practice, von Hansemann ended up withdrawing
her offer of a foundation and investing the money
in a residential and educational facility for women.
The building was called the Viktoria Studienhaus in
tribute to the patronage of Empress Viktoria and
was built from 1914 onward by Emilie Winkelmann.
Shortly after the completion of the Viktoria Studienhaus, Winkelmann and von Hansemann moved into a
coachman's house converted by Winkelmann in the
courtyard of the house at Fraunhoferstrasse 25–27
in Charlottenburg. The modest dimensions of the
building, which have been handed down through historical photographs, suggest that the residents were
living in an arrangement known as a "Boston Mar-
riage," in which two women of independent means —
whether or not romantically involved—set up a household together. As a place of education and residence
for more than one hundred women, the Viktoria Studienhaus reflected the reformist ideas of the women's
movement in an exemplary manner. This also applied
to other Winkelmann designs, such as the "House of
Women" at the Internationale Buchgewerbe-Ausstel-
lung in Leipzig, the Lyceum Klub in Berlin, and the
apartments for retired working women in Potsdam.
However, another network must also be mentioned
here: since Winkelmann refused party membership,
she received no more public commissions after the
National Socialists came to power in 1933.

An Attempt at Appreciation

Emilie Winkelmann was an outstanding personality.
Intelligent, courageous, determined, and open-minded
she asserted herself in a male-dominated field by
studying architecture and practicing it with great
success. Her designs cautiously developed the ruling
canon. She refrained from the Eclecticism that still
prevailed towards the end of the Imperial Era; she
was interested in pragmatic solutions. As a result, her
formal language is more varied than that of her male
competitors. This often translated into greater indi-
viduality and a stronger response to the wishes of the
client, but at the same time lower recognition value.

Architectural critics see the quality of her designs
as being in a league with contemporaries Alfred
Messel or Hermann Muthesius, who are better known
today. However, it must also be noted that Winkelmann
continued to use unchanged the formal language
developed during and for the society of the German
Empire after the end of World War I. It is not enough
to see this as being based solely on the pragmatism
of a service provider. Winkelmann was probably of
interest to the East Elbian nobility until the nineteen-thirties, and even, albeit to a very limited extent,
until the end of her life as an architect, because she
had internalized the spirit of the Empire and still knew
how to implement it in her work. Thus, Winkelmann
did not follow the major developments in architecture
from the nineteen-twenties onward. Serial production,
affordable living space, or the living environment
of the worker were not the subjects of her work. She
did not want to revolutionize society as other early
Modernist architects did: the absence of a "mission"
is certainly chalked up against her work. She employed
excellent craftsmanship, formulated interesting
architectural ideas, and translated these into built
reality—no small accomplishment around 1900, when
society and her chosen profession were dominated
by men. Her biography has made her a promoter of
women's rights and above all of women's access to
education. One hundred years after Walter Gropius
founded the Bauhaus, this is perhaps the most
interesting aspect of her work. Gropius and his Bauhaus: this mission has become a trademark. However,
the fact that even in this undisputed avant-garde
institution, women were by no means able to position themselves as architects—they were considered
best in arts and crafts—speaks for the energetic and
courageous pioneering work of women like Emilie
Winkelmann.

1   Taken from Emilie Winkelmann's
hand-written curriculum vitae of
September 14, 1950, Architectural
Archives of the Berlinische Galerie,
Museum of Modern Art, Berlin.

2   Patricia Mazón, "Das akademische
Bürgerrecht und die Zulassung von
Frauen zu den deutschen Universitäten
1865–1914," in *Zur Geschichte des
Frauenstudiums und Wissenschaftlerinnenkarrieren an deutschen Universitäten*,
ed. Gabriele Jähnert (Berlin, 2001), p. 1.

3   Jarno Jessen, *Angewandte Kunst*
(Berlin, 1908).

4   Despina Stratigakos, "The Professional Spoils of War: German Women
Architects and World War I," in *Journal
of the Society of Architectural Historians*
66 (April 2007), pp. 464–75, doi.org/
10.1525/jsah.2007.66.4.464 (accessed
August 25, 2020).

5   A book with an introduction by
Theodor Heuss, published in 1918,
presents in detail all the designs
submitted for the Haus der Freundschaft
competition: Deutscher Werkbund and
Deutsch-Türkische Vereinigung, *Das
Haus der Freundschaft in Konstantinopel:
Ein Wettbewerb deutscher Architekten*
(Munich, 1918).

Eileen Gray

E.1027

Beatriz Colomina

Eileen Gray

A modern white house is perched on the rocks, a hundred feet above the Mediterranean Sea, in a remote place, Roquebrune at Cap Martin in France. The site is "inaccessible and not overlooked from anywhere."[1] No road leads to this house. It was designed and built between 1926 and 1929 by Eileen Gray for Jean Badovici and herself. Gray named the house E.1027: E for Eileen, 10 for J, the tenth letter of the alphabet, 2 for B and 7 for G. Gray and Badovici lived there most summer months, until Gray built her own house in Castellar in 1934. After Badovici's death in 1956, the house was sold to the Swiss architect Marie-Louise Schelbert. She found the walls riddled with bullet holes. The house had clearly been the scene of some considerable violence. In a 1969 letter, she commented on the state of the house: "Corbu [architect Charles-Édouard Jeanneret, known as Le Corbusier] did not want anything repaired and urged me to leave it as it is as a reminder of war."[2] But what kind of war? Most obviously, it was World War II. The bullet holes were wounds from the German occupation. But what violence was there to the house before the bullets, and even before the inevitable relationship of modern architecture to the military? And anyway, to start with, what was Le Corbusier doing here? What brought him to this isolated spot, this remote house that would eventually be the site of his own death?

We will have to go back to Le Corbusier's earlier travels, to the "strange, inaccessible places and scenes" that he had conquered through drawing at the very least, to Le Corbusier's trip to Algiers in the spring of 1931, the first encounter in what would become a long relationship to this city, or in Le Corbusier's words, "Twelve years of uninterrupted study of Algiers."[3]

By all accounts, this study began with his drawing of Algerian women. He said later that he had been "profoundly seduced by a type of woman particularly well built," of which he made many nude studies.[4] He also acquired a big collection of colored postcards depicting naked women surrounded by accoutrements from the Oriental bazaar. Jean de Maisonseul, later director of the Musée National des Beaux-Arts d'Alger, who as an eighteen-year-old boy had guided Le Corbusier through the Casbah, recalls their tour: "Our wanderings through the side streets led us at the end of the day to the rue Kataroudji where he [Le Corbusier] was fascinated by the beauty of two young girls, one Spanish and the other Algerian. They brought us up a narrow stairway to their room; there he sketched some nudes on—to my amazement— some schoolbook graph paper with colored pencils; the sketches of the Spanish girl lying both alone on the bed and beautifully grouped together with the Algerian turned out accurate and realistic; but he said that they were very bad and refused to show them."[5] Le Corbusier filled three notebooks of sketches in Algiers that he later claimed were stolen from his Paris atelier. But Amédée Ozenfant denies it, saying that Le Corbusier himself either destroyed or hid them, considering them a "secret d'atelier."[6] The Algerian sketches and postcards appear to be a rather ordinary instance of the ingrained fetishistic appropriation of women, of the East, of "the other." Yet Le Corbusier, as Samir Rafi and Stanislaus von Moos have noted, turned this material into "preparatory studies for and the basis of a projected monumental figural composition, the plans for which seem to have preoccupied Le Corbusier during many years, if not his entire life."[7] From the months immediately following his return from Algiers until his death, Le Corbusier seems to have made hundreds and hundreds of sketches on yellow tracing paper by laying it over the original sketches and redrawing the contours of the figures. He also exhaustively studied Delacroix's famous painting *Les Femmes d'Alger dans leur appartement,* producing a series of sketches of the outlines of the figures in this painting, divested of their "exotic clothing" and the "Oriental décor."[8] Soon the two projects merged: he modified the gestures of Delacroix's figures, gradually making them correspond to the figures in his own sketches. Le

Le Corbusier, *Grafitte à Cap Martin,* 1938. Wall painting under the pilotis in the garden hall of E.1027, which Le Corbusier applied without the architect's knowledge or permission.

Le Corbusier, nude while working on a wall painting in E.1027

Eugène Delacroix, *Femmes d'Alger dans leur appartement,* 1834, oil on canvas, 180 × 229 cm. Le Corbusier studied the painting in detail and made numerous sketches.

Corbusier said that he would have called the final composition *Les Femmes de la Casbah.*[9] In fact, he never finished it. Drawing and redrawing these pictures became a lifelong obsession for him, which is a sign that something critical was at stake here. This became even more obvious when in 1963–64, shortly before his death, Le Corbusier, unhappy with the visible aging of the yellow tracing paper, copied a selection of twenty-six drawings onto transparent paper and, symptomatically for someone who kept everything, burned the rest.[10]

But the process of drawing and redrawing the *Les Femmes de la Casbah* reached its most intense, if not hysterical, moment when Le Corbusier's studies found their way into a mural that he completed in 1938 in E.1027. Le Corbusier referred to the mural as *Sous les pilotis* (below the pilotis) or *Graffite à Cap Martin* (graffito in Cap Martin); sometimes he also labeled it *Trois Femmes* (three women).[11] According to Marie-Louise Schelbert, Le Corbusier explained to his friends that 'Badou' (Badovici) was depicted on the right, his friend Eileen Gray on the left; the outline of the head and the hairpiece of the sitting figure in the middle, he claimed, was "the desired child, which was never born."[12] This extraordinary scene, a defacement of Gray's architecture, was perhaps even an effacement of her sexuality. For Gray was openly gay, her relationship to Badovici notwithstanding. And insofar as

Pablo Picasso, *Les Femmes d'Alger (version O),* 1955, oil on canvas, 114 × 146 cm. Inspired after a visit to Le Corbusier in E.1027, Picasso also painted a version of the painting by Delacroix.

Badovici is here represented as one of the three women, the mural may reveal as much as it conceals. Particular if we take into account Le Corbusier's obsessive relationship to this house as manifest in his quasi-occupation of the site after World War II, when he built a small wooden shack, the Cabanon, for himself at the very limits of the adjacent property, right behind Gray's house. He occupied and controlled the site by overlooking it, the cabin being little more than an observation platform.

But the violence of this occupation had already been established when Le Corbusier painted the eight murals in the house without Gray's permission. She considered it an act of vandalism; indeed, as Adam put it, "It was a rape. A fellow architect, a man she admired, had without her consent defaced her design."[13]

The defacement of the house went hand in hand with the effacement of Gray as an architect. When Le Corbusier published the murals in his *Oeuvre complète* (1946) and in *L'Architecture d'aujourd'hui* (1948), Gray's house was referred to as "a house in Cap-Martin"; her name was not even mentioned.[14] Later on, Le Corbusier actually got credit for the design of the house and even for some of its furniture.[15] Today the confusion continues, with many writers attributing the house to Badovici alone or, at best, to Badovici and Gray, and others suggesting that Le Corbusier had collaborated on the project. Gray's name does not figure, even as footnote, in most histories of modern architecture, including the most recent and ostensibly critical ones.

"What a narrow prison you have built for me over a number of years, and particularly this year through your vanity," Badovici wrote to Le Corbusier in 1949 about the whole episode (in a letter that Peter Adam thinks may have been dictated by Gray herself).[16] Le Corbusier's reply is clearly addressed to Gray: "You want a statement from me based on my worldwide authority to show—if I correctly understand your innermost thoughts—to demonstrate 'the quality of pure and functional architecture' which is manifested by you in the house at Cap Martin, and has been destroyed by my pictorial interventions. OK, you send me some photographic documents of this manipulation of pure functionalism ... Also send some documents on Castellar, this U-boat of functionalism; then I will spread this debate in front of the whole world."[17] Now Le Corbusier was threatening to carry the battle from the house into the newspapers and architectural periodicals. But his public position completely contradicted what he had expressed privately.

In 1938, the same year he would go on to paint the mural *Graffite à Cap Martin,* Le Corbusier had written a letter to Gray, after having spent some days in E.1027 with Badovici, in which he acknowledged not only her sole authorship but also how much he liked the house: "I am so happy to tell you how much those few days spent in your house have made me appreciate the rare spirit which dictates all the organization, inside and outside, and gives to the modern furniture—the equipment—such dignified form, so charming, so full of spirit."[18]

Why, then, did Le Corbusier vandalize the very house he loved? Did he think that the murals would enhance it? Certainly not. Le Corbusier had repeatedly stated that the role of the mural in architecture is to "destroy" the wall, to dematerialize it. In a letter to Vladimir Nekrassov in 1932, he wrote: "I admit the mural not to enhance a wall, but on the contrary, as a means to violently destroy the wall, to remove from it all sense of stability, of weight, etc."[19] The mural for Le Corbusier is a weapon against architecture, a bomb. "Why then to paint on the walls ... at the risk of killing architecture?" he asked in the same letter, and then answered, "It is when one is pursuing another task, that of telling stories."[20]

So what, then, is the story that he so urgently needed to tell with *Graffite à Cap Martin*?

We will have to go back once more to Algiers. In fact, Le Corbusier's complimentary letter to Gray, sent from Cap Martin April 28, 1938, bears the letterhead, "Hôtel Aletti Alger." Le Corbusier's violation of Gray's house and identity is consistent with his fetishization of Algerian women. The sketches of the Algerian women were not only re-drawings of live models but also re-drawings of postcards. In fact, the whole mentality of the *Femmes de la Casbah* drawings is photographic. Not only were they made from photographs, but they were developed according to a repetitive process in which the images are systematically reproduced on transparent paper, the grid of the original graph paper allowing the image to be enlarged to any scale. This photographic sensibility becomes most obvious with the murals at Cap Martin. Traditionally, they have been understood as paradigm of Le Corbusier the painter, the craftsman detached from mechanical reproduction, an interpretation to which Le Corbusier himself has contributed with the circulation of that famous photograph of him, naked, working at one of the murals. This is the only official nude image of him and that it had to be here, in this scene, is telling. What is normally overlooked is that *Graffite à Cap Martin* was not conceived on the wall itself. Le Corbusier used an electric projector to enlarge the image of a small drawing onto the two-and-a-half-by-four-meter white wall where he etched the mural in black.

Pablo Picasso, visiting Cap Martin, was so impressed with the mural there that it prompted him to do his own version of the *Femmes d'Alger dans leur appartement*. Apparently Picasso drew Delacroix's painting from memory and was later "frappé" to find out that the figure he had painted in the middle, lying down, with her legs crossed, was not in the Delacroix.[21] It was, of course, *Graffite à Cap Martin* that he remembered, the reclining, crossed-legged women, inviting but inaccessible, Le Corbusier's symptomatic representation of Gray.

The mural was a black-and-white photograph. By drawing he entered the photograph that is itself a stranger's house, occupying and re-territorializing the space, the city, the sexualities of the other by re-working the image. Drawing on and in photography is the instrument of colonization. Entering into the house of a stranger is always a breaking and entering—there being no entry without force no matter how many invitations. Le Corbusier's architecture depends in some way on specific techniques of occupying yet gradually effacing the domestic space of the other. Like all colonists, Le Corbusier did not think of it as an invasion but as a gift. When recapitulating his life's work five years before his death, he symptomatically wrote about Algiers and Cap Martin in the same terms: "From 1930 L-C devoted twelve years to an uninterrupted study of Algiers and its future ... Seven great schemes (seven enormous studies) were prepared *free of charge* during those years"; and later, "1938–9. Eight mural paintings (*free of charge*) in the Badovici and Helen Grey house at Cap Martin."[22] No charge for the discharge. Gray was outraged; now even her name was defaced. And renaming is, after all, the first act of colonization. Such gifts cannot be returned. But who was the gift for, after all? Certainly not for Eileen Gray. The gift was for Le Corbusier himself. This can be seen in the obsessive attempt to keep his own gift.

After the death of Badovici, the property of the house passed to his sister, an elderly nun living in Bucharest who had given powers to the American Adventists taking care of her. Le Corbusier started an extraordinary campaign to control the destiny of the house. He wrote over a hundred elaborate letters and notes to the pastor in charge of selling the house, to friends in Switzerland trying to arrange for a suitable buyer, most notably his publisher Boesiger and gallerist Heidi Weber, to a notary of the Cap Martin area trying to establish the value of the house against the pastor's request for 30 million French francs, to the director of SPADEM requesting that he write a threatening letter to the pastor, advising him of Le Corbusier's intentions to make the preservation of the murals a condition, to the eventual buyer of

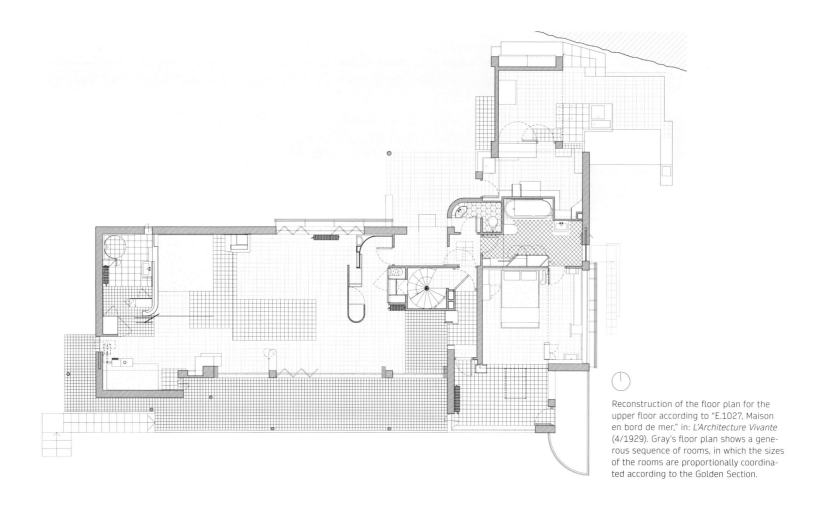

Reconstruction of the floor plan for the upper floor according to "E.1027, Maison en bord de mer," in: *L'Architecture Vivante* (4/1929). Gray's floor plan shows a generous sequence of rooms, in which the sizes of the rooms are proportionally coordinated according to the Golden Section.

The facade facing the sea illustrates the metaphor of nautical architecture: the supports are painted blue on the inside, the steel railing of the balcony is reminiscent of a ship's railing, the sun protection is a kind of tensioned canvas, and the glass exit on the roof resembles a ship's bridge.

the house, the Swiss architect Marie-Louise Schelbert, advising her on what to do and what not to do, including precise instructions on wearing a hat, presumably to make bids at the auction, and so on and on. The letters, sometimes three or more pages long and including drawings, sketches, and photographs, explain in excruciating detail how extraordinary the house and its location are, the neighboring houses, the beach, the other beach, the station connecting it to Bordeaux, Paris, Frankfurt, Geneva, Gênes, Rome … every detail of everyday life down to the perfect cuisine of L'Étoile de mer, the restaurant immediately above E.1027, and eating in the sun on the terrace of Roberto, the owner of L'Étoile de mer.

Most remarkably, a recurring theme appears in all these letters: the fear that the house could be turned into a house of ill repute, a bordello. It is hard to imagine the idea that a modest modern house by the sea on what was by then a very expensive piece of property surrounded by luxurious villas could be turned into a brothel, but Le Corbusier keeps repeating the idea obsessively in numerous letters to all kinds of people: "If the filthy beasts installed a bordello in this house, they will destroy the 8 mural paintings. If your group buys it, they will be saved," he says to Boesiger. These are not just any old images on the wall. They are his life's effort to control the threatening femininity of the material world, to be the master.

Le Corbusier's last success was that E.1027 was bought at auction by the Swiss architect Marie-Louise Schelbert, who was convinced that she was buying a house by Le Corbusier. His wall paintings were "saved."

In 1944, the retreating German Army blew up Gray's apartment in Menton, having vandalized E.1027 and Tempe à Pailla (her house in Castellar). She lost everything. Her drawings and plans were used to light fires. On August 26, 1965, the endless redrawing of the *Femmes de la Casbah* still unfinished, Le Corbusier went down from E.1027 to the sea and swam to his death.

1   Peter Adam, *Eileen Gray: Architect/Designer* (New York, 1967), p. 174.

2   Letter from Marie-Louise Schelbert to Stanislaus von Moos, February 14, 1969, as quoted by von Moos in "Le Corbusier as Painter," *Oppositions* 19–20 (1980), p. 93.

3   Le Corbusier, *My Work,* trans. James Palmer with an introduction by Maurice Jadot (London, 1960), p. 50.

4   Samir Rafi, "Le Corbusier et 'Les Femmes d'Alger,'" *Revue d'histoire et de civilisation du Maghreb* (January 1968), p. 51.

5   Letter from Jean de Maisonseul to Samir Rafi, January 5, 1968, as quoted by Stanislaus von Moos in von Moos 1980 (see note 2), p. 89.

6   From several conversations of both Le Corbusier and Ozenfant with Samir Rafi in 1964. As quoted by Samir Rafi in Rafi 1968 (see note 4), p. 51.

7   Von Moos 1980 (see note 2), p. 91.

8   Idem, p. 93.

9   Rafi 1968 (see note 4), pp. 54–55.

10   Idem, p. 60.

11   In *My Work* (see note 3), Le Corbusier refers to the mural as *Graffiti at Cap Martin.* In "Le Corbusier as Painter," Stanislaus von Moos labels the mural *Three Women (Graffite à Cap Martin),*" and in "Le Corbusier et Les Femmes d'Alger," Samir Rafi labels the final composition from which the mural was derived *"Assemblage des trois femmes: composition définitive.* Encre de Chine sur papier calque. 49.7 × 64.4 cm. Coll. particulière. Milan."

12   Letter from Marie-Louise Schelbert to Stanislaus von Moos, February 14, 1969, as quoted by Von Moos 1980 (see note 2), p. 93.

13   Adam 1967 (see note 1), p. 311.

14   Idem, pp. 334–35. No caption of the photographs of the murals published in *L'architecture d'aujourd'hui* mentions Eileen Gray. In subsequent publications, the house is either simply described as "Maison Badovici" or credited directly to Badovici. The first recognition since the nineteen-thirties of Gray as architect came from Joseph Rykwert, "Un Ommagio a Eileen Gray—Pioniera del Design," *Domus* 468 (December 1966), pp. 23–25.

15   For example, in an article entitled "Le Corbusier, Muralist," published in *Interiors* (June 1948), the caption of the murals at Cap Martin reads: "Murals, interior and exterior, executed in sgraffito technique on white plaster, in *a house designed by Le Corbusier and P. Jeanneret,* Cap Martin, 1938." In 1981, in *Casa Vogue* 119 (Milan), the house is described as "Firmata Eileen Gray—Le Corbusier" (signed Eileen Gray and Le Corbusier), and an Eileen Gray sofa as "pezzo unico di Le Corbusier" (unique piece by Le Corbusier), as quoted by Jean Paul Rayon and Brigitte Loye in "Eileen Gray architetto 1879–1976," *Casabella* 480 (May 1982), pp. 38–42.

16   "Quelle réclusion étroite que m'a faite votre vanité depuis quelques années et qu'elle m'a faite plus particulièrement cette année." Letter from Badovici to Le Corbusier, December 30, 1949, Fondation Le Corbusier, as quoted by Brigitte Loye in *Eileen Gray 1879–1976: Architecture Design* (Paris, 1983), p. 86; English translation in Adam 1967 (see note 1), p. 335.

17   "Vous réclamez une mise au point de moi, couvert de mon autorité mondiale, et démontrant—si je comprends le sens profond de votre pensée—'la qualité d'architecture fonctionnelle pure' manifesté par vous dans la maison de Cap Martin et anéantie par mon intervention picturale. D'ac [sic], si vous me fournissez les documents photographiques de cette manipulation fonctionnelle pure: 'entrez lentement'; 'pyjamas'; 'petites choses'; 'chaussons'; 'robes'; 'pardessus et parapluies'; et quelques documents de Castellar, ce sous-marin de la fonctionnalité: Alors je m'efforcerai d'étaler le débat au monde entier." Letter from Le Corbusier to Badovici, Fondation Le Corbusier, as quoted in Loye 1983 (see note 16), pp. 83–84; English translation in Adam 1967 (see note 1), pp. 335–36.

18   Letter from Le Corbusier to Eileen Gray, Cap Martin, April 28, 1938, as quoted in Adam 1967 (see note 1), pp. 309–10.

19   "J'admets la fresque non pas pour mettre en valeur un mur, mais au contraire comme un moyen pour détruire tumultueusement le mur, lui enlever toute notion de stabilité, de poids, etc." *Le Corbusier, Le passé à réaction poétique,* catalogue of an exhibition organized by the Caisse nationale des Monuments historiques et des Sites/Ministère de la Culture et de la Communication, Paris 1988, p. 75.

20   Ibid: "Mais pourquoi a-t-on peint les murs des chapelles au risque de tuer l'architecture? C'est qu'on poursuivait une autre tâche, qui était celle de raconter des histoires."

21   Rafi 1968 (see note 4), p. 61.

22   Le Corbusier 1960 (see note 3), pp. 50–51 [my emphasis].

Lina Bo Bardi

A Contemporary Legacy

Sol Camacho

Lina Bo Bardi

During my first days of architecture school in 1999, my mom, a practicing architect, gifted me the book *Lina Bo Bardi,* published in 1993. Thus, with two foundational points of reference, I began my studies in Mexico at the very end of the twentieth century believing that women had always had an important role in Latin American architecture.

Today, exactly twenty years later, as a practitioner in twenty-first century Brazil, I cannot imagine what it would have been like had I known the truth, that women in Latin America had (and still have) very little space in the field of architecture.

Lina Bo Bardi, Italian by birth but Brazilian by choice, was the exception. Lina had a strong presence in the cultural and intellectual life of Brazil, from her arrival in the middle of the twentieth century until her death in 1992.

Bo Bardi studied in Rome, which at the time was dominated by conservatives such as Gustavo Giovannoni and Marcello Piacentini, and in a wartime climate with little architectural production. After graduating in 1939, she moved to Milan, which was far more open to modern architecture than the capital, in order to found her own architectural practice together with Carlo Pagani. Later she joined Gio Ponti's office and collaborated with him on the publication of the magazine *Lo Stile nella casa e nell'arredamento.* In 1944 she became deputy director of *Domus,* where she developed editorial projects that allowed her to work and have a voice, even during times of war. In Milan she met Pietro Bardi, at that time an art dealer, gallery owner, and art critic. They married in 1946.

The Bardis traveled to Rio de Janeiro later that year on a commercial venture to sell art. There, Professor Bardi—as Pietro Bardi was known—was introduced to Assis Chateaubriand, a media mogul who supported the arts and had the ambition and vision to build an art museum. The initial meeting with Chateaubriand,

which took place very shortly after the Bardis' arrival in Brazil, turned into a lifetime relationship that would eventually help build the country's cultural identity.

Pietro and Lina settled in São Paulo and, after a short period, in 1949, started plans to build a house. They imagined a house that reflected Lina's ideals of modern architecture, where new uses for industrial materials could be applied in a domestic space. The region of Morumbi, across the river and in the city's outskirts, was starting to be developed as a single-family residential area and was introduced to the couple by the architect Gregori Warchavchik,[1] also a European immigrant and an important figure in the consolidation of modern architecture in Brazil.

Aline Coelho has found that the Bardis initially considered building the house as a cultural center for the Museu de Arte de São Paulo (MASP) design school, a part of the Contemporary Art Institute (IAC). When that plan fell through, the house was left to serve as the couple's residence and would later become the so-called Casa de Vidro ("Glass House").[2,3] Coelho also suggests that the Bardis chose a site close to an original chapel and the former seat of a *fazenda* (estate) of a tea plantation as a way to relate to the history of the place. What I have not found in any document is the reason for choosing a site with such an accentuated topography. However, reading Lina's article "Case sui trampoli,"[4] published in Italy's *Domus* magazine in 1944, one can imagine that she was already thinking of a house standing on pilotis. The steep, hilly site was ideal for a protruding volume—especially a glass volume.

Glass was the perfect material to accentuate the desired lightness; its inherent transparency materialized Lina's idea of a blurred relationship between the exterior and interior. She wrote: "This house represents an attempt to achieve a communion between nature and the natural order of things. By raising minimum defenses against the natural elements,

Glass House, São Paulo, 1951. The house is situated on a slope and consists of two built volumes: the front of the house is supported by slender pilotis, and its continuous glass facade reinforces the floating aspect of this public building tract. The private part at the rear lies on the ground and is built using conventional construction techniques.

43

it tries to respect this natural order, with clarity, and never as a hermetically sealed box that flees from the storms and rain, shies away from the world of men—the kind of box which, on the rare occasions it approaches nature, does so only in a decorative or compositional, and therefore 'external' sense."[5]

While the ideas for the house were mainly Lina's, it is worth nothing that Pietro supported and encouraged the modernist plan. Pietro was an admirer of the modern movement. He had been in contact with Le Corbusier and participated of the Fourth International Congress of Modern Architecture (CIAM) in 1933. As editor of the journal *Il Vetro* (1939–43), a magazine that represented glass and ceramics manufacturer's associations, he had the dual aims of disseminating information and providing the architectural and industrial communities with knowledge and inspiration.[6] As Pietro and Lina were both fascinated with the possibilities of glass, they used the house as an experiment that would later inform the renowned MASP project.

The couple agreed on major concepts of the plan, but it was indisputably Lina's hand that designed every element of the house. In our recent book, *Glass Houses,* Renato Anelli and I describe it thus: "The structural conception of a modular grid for pillars and beams came from Lina: these can be found in her very first renderings. [The structure] served as the basis for a sophisticated project by the Italian engineer Pier Luigi Nervi, a friend of Pietro's since the nineteen-thirties. In Nervi's design, pillars made of cylindrical steel tubes receive steel beams, but when the house was built the availability of steel sections was just scant as was a qualified workforce [to build it]. For this reason, Nervi's project was adapted by Brazilian engineer Tulio Stucci into a version with beams and reinforced concrete slabs, preserving only the modular quality and the slenderness of the original cylindrical pillars."[7]

The glass volume, with its iconic stair, is only half of the house. The modern volume, containing the social portion of the house, is connected to a grounded, standard masonry construction where private life can take place: there we find bedrooms, bathrooms, the kitchen, and staff rooms. Instead of sleek glass panes, there are louvered windows supported by standard hinges. Ascending from the main staircase through the living room, towards the kitchen and through the back door, a visitor makes the transition from Bauhaus to farmhouse. The very back of the house, with a set of rooms for the staff, is a direct echo of the social dynamics of Brazil, a hierarchical, post-colonial condition that is in direct conflict with modernist egalitarianism.

The house changes as it becomes more directly related to the topography. The ample glass rooms

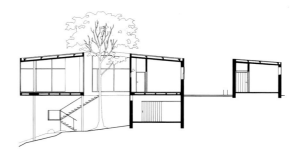

Cross section

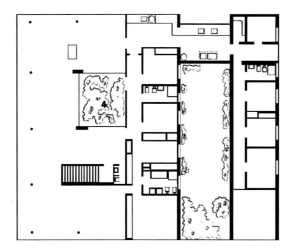

Floor plan, upper floor

are stilted high above the terrain. As it moves closer to the house, however, it eventually reaches the area for the bathrooms, bedrooms, and kitchen, which become a simple masonry and concrete construction supported directly by the ground rather than pilotis.

This duality can be interpreted in many ways: modern and traditional, European and Brazilian, public and private. The fact is that the house allowed for a prolific life of ideas, one shared among a social circle of artists, intellectuals, politicians, architects, gallerists, and friends. The house was famous for its Sunday lunches. Pictures and documents in the couple's archive portray Lina as the hostess of many meals, as well as informal gatherings around the dinner table and in the living room; the guests are often found sitting on furniture she designed specifically for the house.

All of the home's furniture was designed using steel structures. The dining room table, the salon coffee tables, stools, and even the bed and bedside tables were painted blue, merging them with the blue mosaic floor, making them appear almost as if they were floating. The iconic Bola chair and "the Bowl," a semi-spherical seat resting lightly on a metallic ring structure, supported by four legs, were also designed for the house. Lina had previously designed furniture in her Estudio Palma in São Paulo, a joint venture with Italian architect Giancarlo Palanti. Estudio Palma

House and natural surroundings are intertwined: The house is accessed from below via a freestanding staircase from the garden, a tree grows over an inner courtyard as if it were growing through the house, and the continuous glazing of the living space seems to dissolve the boundary between inside and outside.

was critical in Bo Bardi's career as a designer—it was there that she created the MASP auditorium chair, which she declared to be "the first modern chair in Brazil":[8]

"The experimental and exceptionally innovative Estudio Palma was part of a society that was changing, but not as much as the city. The bourgeoisie still chose stylish furniture, specially imported from France or copied from magazines, featuring excessive gilding, draping, and opulent shapes. Introducing modern furniture was slow and very difficult."[9]

Lina's preoccupation with interior design was as strong as her fascination with the home's exterior. The garden that surrounds the house was a continuous project. Early photographs by Peter Scheier and Chico Albuquerque, originally published in national and international magazines, show an open landscape with few trees and vast, grassy hills.[10] In the meantime, this landscape has transformed into the lush tropical garden that today surrounds the house, almost hiding it from view.

During recently completed research on the house funded by the Getty Foundation, the landscape research team led by Luciana Scheck found significant evidence that Lina planted nearly all of the garden and was involved in deciding which species to plant. "Lina's library reveals Lina as a tree-planter; as a collector of botany books, each with handwritten notes on the contents of her herb garden; as an orchid and flower lover. Lina itemized species of vegetation in plant nursery shopping lists. Lina was very aware of another dimension of continental Brazil, as can be seen from the presence of books on its geography and biomes, from the Cerrado scrublands to the Amazon rainforest."[11]

The garden evolved along with Lina's architecture. "The 760 m² Glass House is not the only structure on the 7,000 m² lot. The diversity of the constructions on the site reveals the evolution of Lina's thinking, which underwent many changes as she traveled, studied, and made contact with new concepts and movements in architecture. Despite its discrete and semi-buried settlement, a house designed for the property's caretaker tailgates the main house's construction, keeping up with its modern contours. Both the garden railing and the garage volume seem to have come directly from [Antoni Gaudí's] Park Güell, bearing a strong resemblance to the organicist thought of Bruno Zevi, a colleague and friend. The studio, built in 1986, reflects the admiration for popular architecture and local techniques that Lina developed during her multiple stays in Bahia."[12]

The Glass House, which became an icon of modern architecture, was Lina's first building. When discussing the building later in her life, she often said that were she to build it over again, "she would do it completely different, with other materials, with eaves."[13] It was her lifelong journey in Brazil that brought her to this conclusion: her evolution was one of design and philosophy. She intertwined her preoccupations with social issues with her buildings and her choices of materials, forms, and spaces. As she matured, she became more convinced of the idea that architecture was a social discipline, arguing, "architecture isn't only utopia, but it is a means to reach certain collective results."[14]

In this sense, Lina and her husband left their house as a place to continue their legacy. They went through the efforts of listing the house in all of Brazil's heritage institutions, guaranteeing its future; they founded the Instituto Lina Bo e P.M. Bardi. Instituto Bardi/Casa de Vidro is today an active cultural center: exhibitions of art, architecture, urban planning, graphic and industrial design, and other disciplines are showcased in the Casa de Vidro's various spaces.

Like the Glass House, other buildings by Lina Bo Bardi are places to be inspired. As Isa Grinspum Ferraz mentions in the 1993 documentary on the architect's life and career, "[Lina's] immense will of dreaming and of building a new world, caused her to create such strong work …."[15]

As an architect and a thinker, Lina Bo Bardi challenged the status quo in every project she was involved in; moreover, she did so in a completely male-dominated environment. Her vision drove her to innovate at every level, bringing daring ideas to each piece of work, from the simplest projects (like her workshops for children) to the biggest urban gestures, like the Museu de Arte de São Paulo.

Museo de Arte de São Paulo (MASP), 1968. The exhibition volume was raised with the help of two strong, red concrete brackets in order to keep the first floor free as a public space. Visitors enter the museum from below via a wide, open staircase.

Lina Bo Bardi on the rocking chair she designed in 1948, the so-called Poltrona de Balanço.

When commissioned to build the MASP, she responded boldly by leaving all of its ground floor free for the city to use, its facades transparent to "let in" anyone from the street, and its interior as an ambiguous layered space of spectacle and spectators. More than a unique cultural building, she gave São Paulo a machine for social interaction.

When asked to build a new cultural center for the Serviço Social do Comércio (SESC), she questioned the plans for demolition and instead proposed to stack the program in a new tower, leaving the original structure "untouched."[16] She pioneered in the concept of adaptive reuse, or the conversion of historical buildings, which is today widely used around the world.

When asked to build São Paulo's city hall, she wrote: "this building won't be like common public administration buildings that are closed to the very people they serve. This building will be open to life, it will have children's spaces, a large coffee shop, an exhibition space, an auditorium … the New City Hall will be open to and for the public."

When she wrote, Lina Bo Bardi created spaces even without building; when building, she constructed more than steel and concrete, she constructed social spaces and social connections.

Lina thought differently and her legacy lives on.

1   On Warchavchik, see Jose Lira, *Warchavchik: fraturas da vanguarda* (São Paulo, 2011).

2   Aline Coelho Sanches, "The Glass House: A Worksite for Continuous Experimentation," text and research developed for the Conservation and Management Plan for Instituto Bardi, as part of the Keeping it Modern program funded by the Getty Foundation, 2019.

3   As far as we have been able to verify, the nickname "Glass House" was given to the Bardis' home in Morumbi and used for the first time publicly by Gio Ponti in his article on the house published in the February 1953 issue of *Domus* (see note 9). In the text, he declares that this was the name that residents of the nearby neighborhood used to refer to the house when he visited the previous year. International circulation of the magazine resulted in the name's use in other publications, as well as its adoption by the Bardis themselves, who had initially called it the "Morumbi House." This information was originally published as a footnote in Coelho Sanches 2019 (see note 2).

4   Lina Bo Bardi, "Case sui trampoli," *Domus* (March 1944), p. 195.

5   Lina Bo Bardi, "Residência no Morumbí," *Habitat* 10 (January–March 1953), pp. 31–39.

6   Renato Anelli and Sol Camacho, *Glass Houses* (São Paulo, 2019), p. 79.

7   Idem, p. 81.

8   Anna Carboncini, "Lina Bo Bardi Designer," in *Lina Bo Bardi; Giancarlo Palanti: Studio D'Arte Palma 1948–1951*, ed. Nina Yashar (Milan, 2018), p. 11.

9   Idem, p. 15.

10   See Gio Ponti, "La 'Casa de Vidro,'" *Domus* 279 (February 1953), pp. 19–26; Bo Bardi 1953 (see note 4); Lina Bo Bardi, "Entre o céu e a vegetação pousa a casa de dois artistas," *Revista Casa e Jardim* 1 (May 1953), pp. 8–13.

11   Schenk, Luciana Bongiovanni Martins, Ligía Teresa Paludetto, and André Tostes Graziano. "The Glass House and Its Garden: Inventory and Discoveries." In *Plano de Gestão e Conservação da Casa de Vidro* edited by Renato Anelli. Unpublished. São Paulo, 2018. Text and research developed for the Conservation and Management Plan for Instituto Bardi, as part of the "Keeping It Modern" program funded by the Getty Foundation, 2019.

12   Anelli and Camacho 2019 (see note 6), p. 119.

13   Coelho Sanches 2019 (see note 2).

14   Isa Grinspum Ferraz and Aurélio Michiles, *Lina Bo Bardi*, documentary film, 1993 (Brazil), 47:05 min.

15   Idem.

16   The SESC is a particularly Brazilian institution. These centers are financed by a levy paid by all commercial enterprises in Brazil and are intended especially for their employees, but are open to everyone. The employees have free access to any of the centers in their state and their programs range from dental clinics to sports facilities, exhibition spaces, workshop areas, subsidized restaurants, and theaters, all in the same building (or set of buildings, in the case of SESC Pompéia in a renovated factory with an added tower housing a multistory sports facility).

Vision for Madrid, 1992. The painting illustrates the evolution of Madrid as a slow-motion explosion, as a series of expansions, breaking city walls. Zaha's vision continues the explosion on an accelerating trajectory, proposing a linear city that expands towards the airport.

Zaha Hadid

The Functional Rationality of Zaha Hadid's
Radical Formal Innovations

Patrik Schumacher

Zaha Hadid

The formal innovations from the nineteen-eighties and -nineties owe much to the radical, formal, iconoclastic innovations delivered by the early work of Zaha Hadid. What were the major expansionary moves that Zaha gifted to our discipline? We can identify and distinguish four wholly original and empowering "discoveries": Explosion, Calligraphy, Distortion, and Landscape. The design moves indicated by these concepts were so radical that they seemed utterly surreal or absurd at first. (I guess that is why nobody else had ever hit upon them before.) They are expansions of the formal repertoire, and thus might initially be viewed as artistic moves—indeed, they first showed up in Zaha's often-conceptual, rather obscure, seemingly utterly abstract drawings and paintings. However, in the hands of a designing architect, a formal repertoire is always also a problem-solving repertoire, addressing the problems of spatial organization and morphological articulation in the service of the prospective building's social and technical functioning. An expanded formal repertoire delivers an enriched problem-solving toolbox. Hence, we need to comprehend and discuss the new moves together with their empowering affordances—affordances that are indeed congenial to the requirements and desires of our time and are thus potentially able to deliver momentous advantages. Of course, we should not expect these advantages to become fully manifest in the early explorations, but they have started to become manifest in our major mature works of recent years (and I would argue that they promise further compelling manifestations):

Explosion

The surreal move of treating explosion as a compositional strategy soon reveals its power when a plan is no longer a closed and rigid array of nested boxes but a centrifugal force field that is eminently permeable, varied, yet ordered through the directed and progressive expansion of all fragments in relation to the implied point of origin. This dynamic and lawful fragmentation of the plan was a decisive step forward from the random, disordered fragmentation proposed by Deconstructivism. However, the explosion delivers more order than just random fragmentation. It delivers a lawfully differentiated field where the fragments' directionality points back to their shared origin and where the increasing spacing of fragments also indicates their relative position in the field.

Metropolis, 1988. With the sketch of
the Greater London cityscape, Zaha
explores calligraphic fluidity on an urban
scale. The dynamic, pulsating line of
the river gives shape and character to
the city. Accordingly, the urban grid
deforms dynamically.

Calligraphy

The surreal move of translating the dynamism of rapid calligraphic sketching literally (by hard-lining them using an expansive range of "French curves" or "ship curves") into an architectural drawing that is then read as an intended geometry to be built, rather than treating the pulsing curvature of a rapid sketch as a rough, accidental indication of an ideal geometric form meant to be rationalized into straight lines and arcs. Zaha's intricately variegated curves offer more adaptive versatility to push into irregular sites or bulge to give room to internal requirements where needed. Further, as a function of the changing centrifugal force of the rapid hand's/pen's acceleration and deceleration, the curves and curvilinear compositions display lawful and coherent trajectories that we can recognize as coherent and legible figures, each with its own poise, dynamism, or degree of fluidity. This increases legibility and navigability in the face of unavoidable programmatic diversity and complexity.

Distortion

The surreal move of using perspectival projection not to depict regular forms but to create and posit distorted forms. Zaha built up pictorial spaces within which multiple perspective constructions were fused into a seamless dynamic texture. One way to understand these images is as attempts to emulate the experience of moving through an architectural composition, revealing a succession of rather different points of view. Another, more radical way of reading these canvases is to abstract from the implied views and to read the distorted forms as a peculiar architectural world in its own right, with its own characteristic forms, compositional laws, and spatial effects. Usually these compositions are polycentral and multidirectional. All of these features are the result of using multiple, interpenetrating perspective projections. Often, the dynamic intensity of the overall field is increased by using curved instead of straight projection lines. The projective geometry allows us to bring an arbitrarily large and diverse set of elements under its cohering law of diminution and distortion.

MAXXI, Museum of XXI Century Arts, Rome, Italy, 2010. The freedom of the calligraphic hand and its faithful translation demonstrates its empowering, adaptive versatility in this winning scheme and in its final realization.

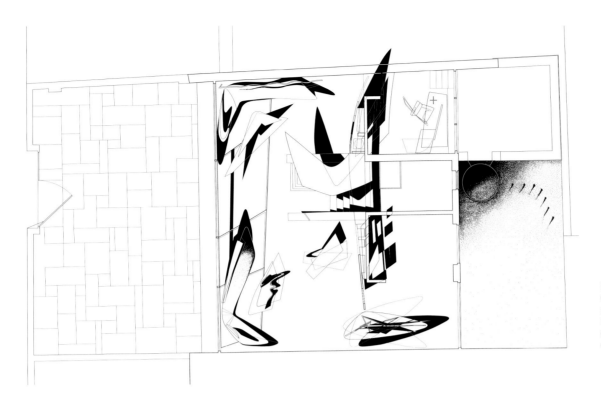

Plan drawing for an interior project in Cathcart Road in London, 1987. The project is one of Hadid's earliest projects, based predominantly on curves with continuously varying radii. It is a good example of her architectural calligraphy.

The resultant graphic space very much anticipates the later (and still very much current) concepts of *field* and *swarm*. The effect achieved is very much like the effects later pursued with digitally simulated "gravitational fields" that distort a mesh or grip, align, orient, and thus integrate a set of elements or particles within the digital model.

Landscape

Instead of dissecting and ordering space with walls, the landscape analogy suggests a continuously flowing space where transitions are soft, where zones are gradually differentiated and bleed into each other, and where a smooth topographic ground relief, rather than hard edges, structures spatial relations. This opens up a whole new ontology of spatial and territorial definition, no longer premised on outline but on a modulated internal texture. We are talking of fields rather than spaces. In contrast to (empty) spaces, fields (like a forest) are full, filled with a modulated medium: i.e., structured via continuously differentiated field conditions so that navigation can follow various vectors of gradual field transformation, such as density or directionality, rather than only orienting by tracking boundary crossings. Zaha's painterly techniques, such as color modulations, fading effects, and pointillism, also reinforce this new ontology of blurred boundaries and soft transitions, which is congenial to contemporary social life and institutions in which the formerly strict distinctions of social classes and arenas are blurred, and domains of competence interpenetrate and bleed into each other.

Through these congenial and empowering repertoire expansions, a new language of architecture with a greatly increased versatility (and thus problem-solving capacity) and a much richer, more expressive, and more communicative repertoire of organization and articulation (and thus ordering capacity) was born. The writings of American formalists such as Jeffrey Kipnis und Greg Lynn delivered a congenial terminology for the verbal articulation of our work. This explicit conceptual articulation is important, as it focuses attention and directs further innovative thrust. The relationship between theory and creative practice is a progressive, dialectical back-and-forth rather than a hierarchical sequence.

Vitra Fire Station, Weil am Rhein, 1993. This design uses isometric and perspectival distortion as design moves that help fit the project into a contextual trajectory and deliver observer-dependent visual effects that animate the spatial experience.

Dongdaemun Design Plaza, Seoul, South Korea, 2013. This project displays the versatility of calligraphic freedom, in which the outline of the project can fit into an irregularly shaped site. The landscape analogy becomes almost literal as park and building interweave and fuse into a coherent, continuous spatial system.

Denise Scott Brown in Las Vegas, 1966

Women in Architecture Today

Ursula Schwitalla

"Architecture is no longer a man's world. This idea that women cannot think three-dimensionally is ridiculous."[1] It was Zaha Hadid who said this to the audience when receiving a prize and thus identified one of many stubborn prejudices against which she had to struggle during her professional life, like many other women architects in the decades and centuries before her. That women and men were evaluated different in their achievements and competencies, even when there was no objective reason for doing so, is one of the many reasons why women architects are still underrepresented in leading positions in academia and in public perception—even though they have had access to education for a century now, and in the meanwhile more than half of all architecture students in Germany are women.[2] Structurally anchored mechanisms that make it more difficult or even impossible for women to enter and rise in the profession, and a male elite leadership whose presence has been reproduced in the media since time immemorial reinforce the discrimination and lack of visibility of women in architecture.

According to the report of the Association of Collegiate Schools of Architecture (ACSA), the proportion of female students in architecture at US and Canadian universities was 44 % in 2015. In professional life, women now account for only 25 % and only 17 % have started their own office.[3]

Share of Academic Staff per Gender in the Faculty of Architecture at TU Munich 2014–16

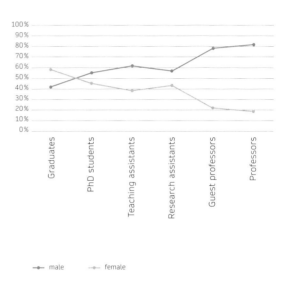

—•— male   —•— female

The figures from 2014–16 show the typical academic path of female architects. Women are in the majority from the start of their studies to the end of their studies. From the doctorate onwards, the picture is reversed and shows the highest divergence between men and women at the professorial level.[4]

Share of Women in Architecture in the US per Career Step

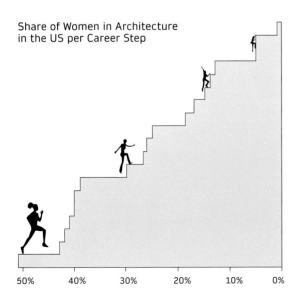

AIA Gold Medals
Pritzker Prizes
AIA/ACSA Topaz Medallions
IDP Supervisors
ACSA Distinguished Professors
Licensed AIA Members
AIA Member Principals and Partners
Deans
Architect Employment
Lecture Series Speakers
School Directors, Heads, and Chairs
AIA Associate Members
NCARB Record Applicants
IDP Interns
ARE Test Takers
Architecture Degrees (all levels)
Accredited Architecture Degrees
Architecture Students
US Population

Where Are the Women Architects?

Women want to become architects, and not just a few of them. The number of women graduates in architecture is nearly at parity in Europe and the United States. But only a fraction of them end up in leading positions. Where are the women architects?

The lack of women role models as teachers, guest critics, and practitioners may have led to women not even risking a professional career. In Germany, only 14 percent of teachers are women and just 5 percent of the chairs at universities are held by women. This is only partially explained by the fact that academic teaching staffs are not primarily qualified by scholarly work as they are in other academic professions but

Share of Female and Male Full- and
Part-Time Employees in Germany 2015

Interruption of Professional Careers
among Architects in Germany

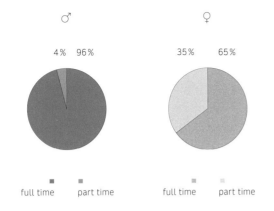

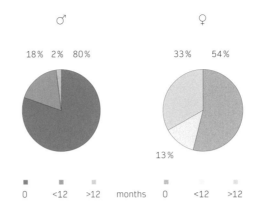

The statistics on full- and part-time work, as well as on career interruptions, indicate a career break among female architects, which can presumably be traced back to pregnancy and starting a family.[8]

come from the "professional elite"; that is, they are recruited from practicing architects. And this elite consists primarily of men.

The practice of the profession is based on highly traditional, male-coded values. The myth of the architect as artistic genius who is completely devoted to the profession and subordinates his entire private life to it is still widespread. The combination of family and profession is irreconcilable with this picture. Part-time positions are therefore largely inconceivable. Although many Western countries are dominated by a self-image that men and women have equal rights, in daily life it is often still the case that tasks are distributed in gender-specific ways: the man brings home the money as the (main) provider, while the woman dedicates herself to unpaid "care work." Even if many women wish to continue working despite having started a family, they often fail for lack of opportunities and support from the professional and governmental side.

The differences between men and women in salary structures reinforce this trend: when a woman earns less than her life partner, it encourages the decision in which he remains active professionally while she takes care of the family and household. According to statistics from the Bundesarchitektenkammer from 2018,[5] women in architectural firms earn on average one quarter less than their male colleagues.[6] In the commercial construction business, they earn 27 percent less for work of the same time and duration. The differences in income increase as age increases, which suggests that women architects end their careers after establishing a family.[7]

All of these mechanisms lead to the result that women do not reach leading positions in architectural offices or academia but necessarily take other paths. They take positions in government offices, where they can count on more support for their

effort to unite career and family. Others venture into self-employment in order to work independently and according to their own rules. Some leave architecture entirely and work in a different field. A large number remain employed in architectural firms in the shadow of the largely male leadership elite.

Women as an exceptional phenomenon in the profession are observed and evaluated particularly critically; more is demanded of them than technical competence: for example, by the juries, which are still predominantly male, by the clients, who are rarely female, by public committees, and finally on the building site itself. All the more so because the theory and methods of architecture are not standardized—and that which manifests itself as quality in architecture is today still determined by a small and almost exclusively male circle. And there is the well-known tendency of stakeholders to opt for those who are similar to them.

The Toxic Cult around Star Architects

The centuries-old picture of the genius architect who thinks, designs, and builds alone has led to most buildings and designs being attributed to a single architect, while the team involved is ignored. This distortion of reality (since not even a moderately complex building can be designed and built by a single person) also leads to the contribution of women architects in particular being ignored. However, this image has ossified into such a strong narrative that cities even make use of it to improve their image: Who wouldn't like to have a male star architect design a building, given the economic success promised by the Bilbao effect?

The media contribute to this cult by producing and reproducing a distorted reality. As a rule, reports tend to speak of the (usually male) head of an office, thus attaching the project to one responsible party rather than speaking of a team. Even when the media do report on office partnerships, the women's names often go unmentioned. How long will it take until all levels of society realize that the famous Weissenhof Chair was actually designed by Lilly Reich (p. 25) and should no longer be attributed to Ludwig Mies van der Rohe? Why have impressive partnerships—such as that of Alison and Peter Smithson in England, who shared responsibility equally for both their architectural projects and the raising of their three children—been received with so little acclaim? And why was Charles Eames, who emphasized often enough that everything he could do his wife, Ray, could do even better, unable to inspire any male architects to express themselves in equally appreciative ways about their female partners and colleagues?

That the me-too debate has also arrived on the architectural scene shows that the unjust treatment of women in architecture goes beyond prejudices and structural mechanisms of exclusion. In 2018, a blacklist of male architects who had been accused of harassing female colleagues, similar to a list circulating in the media sector at the time, was published online. These accusations show the dramatic consequences that unequal power relations between men and women can have. The me-too debate was not without consequences. In March 2018, when several women employees accused Richard Meier of sexual harassment in the *New York Times*, one of the most

popular star architects resigned his position in his own studio.[9] Only when women architects are respected not primarily as women but as colleagues with equal and full rights will such headlines cease.

No Recognition without Prizes

The number of international prizes for architects awarded to women is marginal. Women architects only began to win prizes at all in the nineteen-eighties and in 2010, the ratio of architectural prizes awarded to men and women, respectively, in the United States was 82 to 18 percent.[10] The Gold Medal of the American Institute of Architects (AIA) has been awarded a hundred times since 1907, and in 2014 it was awarded, albeit posthumously, to a woman for the first time: the American architect Julia Morgan (p. 17), who had died fifty-seven years earlier. Two years later, another American woman architect, Denise Scott Brown, received the AIA Gold Medal, this time together with her partner, Robert Venturi. Another internationally respected architectural prize, and the world's oldest, the Royal Gold Medal of the Royal Institute of British Architects (RIBA) was awarded exclusively to men for 150 years before it went to a woman architect, with her partner, for the first time in 1979: Ray Eames received the prize together with Charles Eames for their outstanding teamwork in architecture and design. Only four other women have received it since: Patricia Hopkins (with her partner, Michael Hopkins, 1994), Zaha Hadid (2016), and Yvonne Farrell and Shelley McNamara (2020). Only four women have received the highest honor for architecture, the Pritzker Prize, in the forty-one years of its existence: Zaha Hadid (2004), Kazuyo Sejima (2010), and the cocurators of the Venice Biennale of Architecture in 2018: Yvonne Farrell and Shelley McNamara (2020).[11]

Denise Scott Brown, coauthor of a classic work of architectural theory, *Learning from Las Vegas* (1972), was denied the Pritzker Prize in 1991 when it was awarded exclusively to her partner, Robert Venturi. Venturi's request that she be recognized as well was rejected by the jury. Whereas Denise Scott Brown publicly protested this decision through her absence from the awards ceremony, he nevertheless accepted the prize. Twenty-two years later, the subject would be raised again in 2013, when an international petition on behalf of Denise Scott Brown called for the Pritzker Prize, which had been awarded to Robert Venturi alone in 1991, to be awarded to her as well belatedly—once again the jury refused to do so with the justification that on principle it did not award prizes retroactively.[12]

The Pritzker Prize was awarded to an office partnership for the first time in 2010. Kazuyo Sejima (SANAA) insisted that her office partner Ryūe Nishizawa, who is ten years younger than her, should also be honored.

Yvonne Farrell and Shelley McNamara of Grafton Architects and curators of the Architecture Biennale 2018 in Venice were both winners of the Pritzker Prize in 2020. Along with Patricia Hopkins and her partner Michael Hopkins (1994) and Zaha Hadid (2016), they were also winners of the RIBA Royal Gold Medal.

When the Pritzker Prize was awarded to the Chinese architect Wang Shu of Amateur Architecture Studio, it had a strange twist of its own: not he but his studio and life partner, Lu Wenyu, did not wish to share the prize, since "in China one loses one's life when one becomes famous," she declared in 2013 in her first and only public interview.[13]

The French Association for Research about City and Housing (ARVHA), founded in 1993, aims to promote studies on the theme of the city and housing, sustainability, and equality in architecture. As a logical consequence, since 2013 ARVHA has organized the Prize Woman Architect and the Prize Young Woman Architect, which is open to all women registered with the French Board of architects. The first prizewinner was Odile Decq. Since 2017, an additional international prize for female architects outside of France has been awarded.[14]

The visibility of women in architecture goes hand and hand with their public recognition. The ratio of architectural prizes awarded to men and women today is around 80 to 20 percent, respectively, as noted above. If we project the growing number of architects who have won prizes since the nineteen-eighties, we will have to wait until 2080 to finally achieve parity. Awards granted to women alone could certainly accelerate that. The Women in Architecture prize has been awarded since 2011 by the *Architectural Review* and *Architects' Journal*; in 2020, it was renamed the W Award. In addition, the Architectural Record's Women in Architecture Award in the United States has existed since 2014. The arcVision Prize for women architects in Italy, founded by the Italicementi Group, was only awarded from 2014 to 2016, because it was eliminated when the corporate group was sold to HeidelbergCement in 2017. Germany still does not have a prize for women architects.

Creating Visibility

Since 1980, every two years one of the largest and most influential architectural biennials in the world is held in Venice. The International Architecture Exhibition is distinguished in particular by its reflection on architecture as a broad discipline that influences society. It has only been curated by women twice thus far: in 2010 by the Japanese architect Kazuyo Sejima and in 2018 by Yvonne Farrell and Shelley McNamara, the two architects of the Irish firm Grafton Architects. Hashim Sarkis, the curator of the Venice Biennale of Architecture in 2020, which has been postponed until 2021 because of the coronavirus, called for a reevaluation in his curator's statement: "In the context of widening political divides and growing economic

inequalities, we call on architects to imagine spaces in which we can generously live *together*."[15] The curators of the German Pavilion have also taken up his words and emphasized that only through communal, holistic approaches can architects contribute to the positive development of our coexistence. These words certainly sound motivational, especially with respect to the position of women, but not one of the four curators is a woman. Only in the extended team for the project do the names of the women scholars, artists, and architects involved appear.

Networks for the Future

Recently, important publications on women architects have appeared that testify to a growing interest in the women's work in architecture.[17] They include online platforms such as Madame Architect, founded by the young American architect Julia Gamolina, which has presented women architects from different countries in more than a hundred interviews since 2015.[18]

To improve the visibility of women, it would be worthwhile to have a comprehensive, international database providing the names, dates, and works of women architects. In 1985, the International Archive of Women in Architecture (IAWA) was founded at Virginia Tech University in the United States.[19] The archive collects designs and documents from women architects internationally in order to preserve them for posterity and also make them accessible online. The archive now has the papers of 450 women architects,

Farshid Moussavi, Odile Decq, and Martha Thorne (from left to right) during the flash mob at the Architecture Biennale 2018 in Venice. The demand for fairness, transparency, and collaboration was set down in writing in a manifesto by women architects and read out by Martha Thorne, managing director of the Pritzker Prize, during a flash mob with more than a hundred women architects from all over the world:

"We as Voices of Women are building conversations and taking actions to raise awareness to combat pervasive prejudices and disrespectful behavior that appears to be systemic in our culture and discipline. We are united in denouncing discrimination, harassment, and aggressions against any member of our community. We will not tolerate it. We will not stand silent. Women are not a minority in the world, but women are still a minority in the architecture field and we want it to better reflect the world in which we live.

The Venice Architecture Biennale 2018 FREESPACE is a crucial moment of awakening to promote equitable and respectful treatment of all members of the architectural community irrespective of gender, race, nationality, sexuality, and religion. We will join hands with co-workers, students, clients, collaborators, and our male colleagues to create a new path forward toward equitable work and educational environments that promote respectful discourse and open exchange of ideas.

Be a fan of voices of women. Make a vow to uphold fairness, transparency, and collaboration in Architecture NOW."[16]

Statistical Data from Women Architects World Map 2020

Main Sources

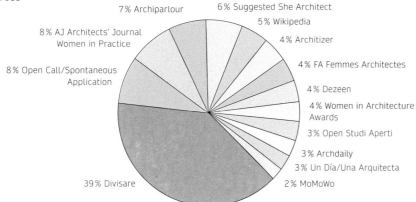

7% Archiparlour
6% Suggested She Architect
5% Wikipedia
8% AJ Architects' Journal Women in Practice
4% Architizer
8% Open Call/Spontaneous Application
4% FA Femmes Architectes
4% Dezeen
4% Women in Architecture Awards
3% Open Studi Aperti
3% Archdaily
3% Un Día/Una Arquitecta
39% Divisare
2% MoMoWo

Team Constellation in Architecture Firms

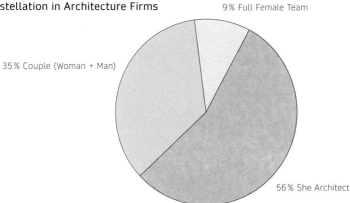

9% Full Female Team
35% Couple (Woman + Man)
56% She Architect

Location of Architecture Firms Worldwide

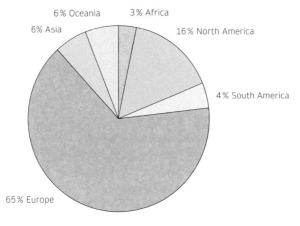

6% Oceania
3% Africa
6% Asia
16% North America
4% South America
65% Europe

By August 2020, the online map of Rebelarchitette had documented 732 female architects worldwide working independently, in partnership with a male architect, or in an all-female team. The map is a collective project to improve the visibility of women in architecture.[22]

a third of which have yet to be published. Since 2001, the IAWA has awarded the annual Milka Bliznakov Research Prize to support historical research on women in architecture.

In Europe, the online research project "MoMoWo: Women's Creativity since the Modern Movement" was created in 2014 as a collaboration among six European universities, with financial support from the European Union.[20] The goal of the project is to share with others the important European cultural heritage created by women in design professions that has largely been "hidden from history,"[21] and to increase awareness of women's work in the design professions.

Contemporary works by European women in the fields of architecture, construction engineering, interior design, landscape architecture, and urban planning will be made available digitally in a database and presented in workshops, publications, exhibitions, and symposia. The project is directed by Emilia Maria Garda, who teaches at the Politecnico di Torino.

One of the most recent online platforms, Rebel-archititette, was founded in 2017 by Francesca Perani of Italy to present one architecture firm run by a woman on each of the 365 days of the year. This activist, collective project has since been published as an e-book: *Architette=Women architects—Here we are!* and was presented at the Venice Architecture Biennale in 2018. Since 2020, all 7 of 106 chambers of architects in Italy (Naples, Rome, Lecce, Turin, Milan, Udine, and Bergamo) have officially accepted the term "Architetta" for professional women architects. A continuously updated world map lists

Location of Architecture Firms per European Country

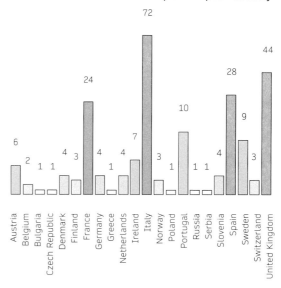

Austria 6
Belgium 2
Bulgaria 1
Czech Republic 1
Denmark 4
Finland 3
France 24
Germany 4
Greece 1
Netherlands 4
Ireland 7
Italy 72
Norway 3
Poland 1
Portugal 10
Russia 1
Serbia 1
Slovenia 4
Spain 28
Sweden 9
Switzerland 3
United Kingdom 44

architectural studios headed by women and thus makes this information available to institutes, universities, and media.

Exhibitions can make an essential contribution to shifting the focus to women. From September 2018 to February 2019, the Deutsches Architekturmuseum (DAM) in Frankfurt am Main presented portraits of twenty-two German women architects under the title *Frau Architekt* (Ms. Architect). Before this exhibition, more than a generation had passed since the first exhibition on the history of women architects and designers in Germany was shown in 1984 on the occasion of the seventh Internationaler Kongress der Architektinnen, Städteplanerinnen und Landschaftsplanerinnen (International Congress of Women Architects, Urban Planners, and Landscape Planners) in Berlin. It was on view for just nineteen days, however. For 2021, the Berlin network of women architects and planners, n-ails Women in Architecture 2021 (WIA), is planning the first festival for women in architecture in Berlin with the motto "Baustelle Gleichstellung/Equality under Construction." For four weeks, it will be a platform for engaging the works of women architects and undertaking a long overdue renovation of the image of the profession.[23]

This also includes the naming of female architects in professional associations. The oldest representation for architects in Germany, the Association of German Architects (BDA), exists since 1903 and according to its own website, unites "5,000 freelance architects, town planners, who stand for quality and personal integrity." The proportion of female members is around 15 percent. It took until 2020 for female architects to be admitted, at least in the name of the Association. Even in 2020, some individual state associations still rejected the amendment to the statutes.

Thirty-Six Women Architects and Their Projects

In her personal interviews with international architects, Tanja Kullak was able to identify an attitude shared by women architects: designing and building architecture means teamwork, and self-promotion is not important.[24] Encounters with the participants in the "Architecture Today" lecture series at the Universität Tübingen confirmed this. The uncomplicated and spontaneous willingness to share their personal experiences resulted in an overwhelming response to the lectures given under the theme Women in Architecture and gave the audience the opportunity to discover the diversity of the work of contemporary women artists.

When the Danish architect Dorte Mandrup (p. 136) emphasized in Tübingen that she sees herself not as a "female architect" but as an "architect," it is perhaps due to the implementation of equal rights being further advanced in Scandinavia compared to Europe and the rest of the world, and the fact that the English word "architect" is ungendered. The website of the Danish firm Lundgaard & Tranberg Arkitekter (p. 184), where the individual has completely receded into the background in favor of presenting the team, could scarcely demonstrate this any better. Of all the participants in the lecture series, one architect from Finland declined to take part in the publication: "in my opinion architects should not be put in groups by their gender—architecture is a group work." If only this practice were widespread all over the world.

For all of the women architects invited who work in office partnerships, it went without saying that their partners should be identified and was a precondition for their participation in the publication: Amateur Architecture Studio (p. 132), Barkow Leibinger (p. 128), Delugan Meissl Associated Architects (p. 72), Annette Gigon/Mike Guyer Architekten (p. 84), Silvia Gmür Reto Gmür Architekten (p. 88), Koning Eizenberg Architecture (p. 76), Lacaton & Vassal Architectes with Frédéric Druot (p. 124), Kazuyo Sejima + Ryūe Nishizawa/SANAA (p. 164), Sunder-Plassmann Architekten (p. 180), and Tod Williams Billie Tsien Architects and Partners (p. 188).

The projects, which the architects have personally selected for this publication, demonstrate the range of their interests, ideas, and tasks they have set themselves. It is striking that nearly two-thirds of the projects can be categorized in the cultural sphere. They are impressive buildings for museums, universities, libraries, cinemas, and conference centers with innovative designs, convincing formal idioms, and high aesthetic ambitions.

Some women architects acknowledge an obligation to society, such as Fabienne Hoelzel, with her participatory neighborhood project in Lagos, Nigeria (p. 108), or Rozana Montiel, with her design for public squares in Mexico, which were developed by the architect in collaboration with their users (p. 140). More cost-effective and less technical construction is another concern, represented by the low-tech house by Anupama Kundoo in Auroville, India (p. 120). In Europe, too, women architects are searching for new, less expensive materials: for example, in the experimental housing of Elisa Valero in Granada, Spain (p. 192).

That the social housing of the postwar era can be adapted to today's needs instead of being demolished is impressively demonstrated by Anne Lacaton and Jean-Philippe Vassal with Frédéric Druot in their renovation of an apartment building in Saint-Nazaire (p. 124). Kathrin Moore presents a project in Da Nang, Vietnam, that is the only urban planning work in this series (p. 144).

It is interesting that nearly half of the projects presented resulted from public competitions. As an anonymized process, this way of allocating contracts ensures a decision that is unaffected by the fame, sex, gender, skin color, or religion of the participants.

Thirty-six great women architects who have successfully ventured the step into independence are presented in this publication along with their projects. This makes visible and pays tribute to their professional commitment and contribution to the culture of architecture. Together with new networks, publications, awards, and festivals that offer platforms for women in architecture, *Women in Architecture* sees itself as a contribution to a more diverse, more accurate picture of the architectural landscape. This book is intended not least to offer younger generations female role models, to give them the courage to take up this wonderful profession.

1   In 2013, Zaha Hadid received the Veuve Clicquot Business Woman Award. This quotation is from her acceptance speech on the awarding of the prize in London and can be heard (at minute 4:25) in this video: www.youtube.com/watch?v=V-n2DgBeQok (accessed September 3, 2020).

2   In Germany, the percentage of women students in architecture in 2019 was as high as 55 % and 57 % of graduates. They only represented 35 % of practicing architects, however. See Statistisches Bundesamt, "Studierende nach dem ersten angegebenen Studienfach," www.bak.de/w/files/bak/07-daten-und-fakten/ausbildung/studierende_architektur_bisss2019.pdf (accessed August 31, 2020) and "Bundeskammerstatistik nach Geschlechtern, Stand 1.1.2020," *Bundesarchitektenkammer,* https://www.bak.de/w/files/bak/07-daten-und-fakten/architektenbefragungen/bundeskammerstatistik/bundeskammerstatistik-nach-geschlechtern-zum-01.01.2020.pdf (accessed August 31, 2020).

3   Lian Chikako Chang, "Where Are the Women? Measuring Progress on Gender in Architecture," *ACSA* (October 2014, www.acsa-arch.org/resources/data-resources/where-are-the-women-measuring-progress-on-gender-in-architecture/ (accessed August 31, 2020).

4   Susanne Ihsen et al., eds., *Frauen in der Architektur: Vorstudie zur Entwicklung eines drittmittelfinanzierten Forschungsprojektes über fachkulturell relevante geschlechtergerechte Veränderung in der Architektur* (Munich, 2018), mediatum.ub.tum.de/doc/1519783/1519783.pdf (accessed August 31, 2020), p. 13.

5   See "Struktur- und Gehaltsanalyse der Architekten und Planer 2018. Repräsentative Befragung der Kammermitglieder 2018 für das Berichtsjahr 2017," Bundesarchitektenkammer, October 6, 2019, www.bak.de/w/files/bak/07-daten-und-fakten/architektenbefragungen/gehaltsumfrage/bak-broschuere-mitgliederbefragung2018endfassung.pdf (accessed August 31, 2020).

6   See "Geschlechterverteilung der Architekten und Stadtplaner in Deutschland in den Jahren von 2012 bis 2020," *statista,* June 23, 2020, de.statista.com/statistik/daten/studie/37278/umfrage/geschlechterverteilung-bei-architekten/ (accessed August 31, 2020).

7   Ihsen 2018 (see note 4).

8   Ihsen 2018 (see note 4), figs. 4.1.4 and 4.1.5.

9   Allison Arieff, "Where Are All the Female Architects?," *The New York Times,* December 15, 2018, www.nytimes.com/2018/12/15/opinion/sunday/women-architects.html (accessed August 25, 2020).

10   Chang 2014 (see note 3).

11   In recent years, the number of Pritzker Prizes awarded to curators of the Venice Architecture Biennale has declined significantly. See, for example, Kaye Geipel, "Die Architekturbiennale wagt den Social Turn," *Bauwelt,* www.bauwelt.de/themen/Die-Architekturbiennale-wagt-den-Social-Turn-Alejandro-Aravena-Biennale-Venedig-2579655.html (accessed August 31, 2020).

12   Rose Etherington, "Denise Scott Brown Petition for Pritzker Recognition Rejected," *Dezeen*, June 14, 2013, www.dezeen.com/2013/06/14/pritzker-jury-rejects-denise-scott-brown-petition/ (accessed August 31, 2020).

13   Anatxu Zabalbeascoa, "La arquitecta que renunció al Pritzker para evitar la fama," in *El País,* October 1, 2013, www.elpais.com/cultura/2013/09/30/actualidad/1380569553_963993.html (accessed August 20, 2020).

14   See www.femmes-archi.org/en (accessed September 9, 2020).

15   Hashim Sarkis, "Introduction," https://www.labiennale.org/en/architecture/2020/introduction-hashim-sarkis (accessed September 7, 2020).

16   "Manifesto for Women in Architecture to Be Read at Venice Biennale," *The Architect's Newspaper,* May 25, 2018, www.archpaper.com/2018/05/manifesto-women-voices-venice-biennale/ (accessed August 31, 2020).

17   See Literature and Sources in this book, p. 213.

18   See www.madamearchitect.org (accessed August 31, 2020).

19   "International Archive of Women in Architecture (IAWA)," in: *Virginia Tech University Libraries,* spec.lib.vt.edu/iawa (accessed August 31, 2020).

20   See www.momowo.eu (accessed August 31, 2020).

21   "The project aims to share significant European Cultural Heritage forged by women working within the design professions, which has been to a significant extent 'hidden from history.'" See "What is MoMoWo?," MoMoWo: Women's Creativity since the Modern Movement, www.momowo.eu (accessed September 2, 2020).

22   See www.rebelarchitette.it (accessed August 31, 2020).

23   See www.n-ails.de (accessed August 31, 2020).

24   Tanja Kullack, *Architecture: A Woman's Profession* (Berlin, 2011), p. 20 ff. and p. 74 ff.

Mona Bayr

Odile Decq

Elke Delugan-Meissl

Julie Eizenberg

Manuelle Gautrand

Annette Gigon

Silvia Gmür

Cristina Guedes

Melkan Gürsel

Itsuko Hasegawa

Anna Heringer

Fabienne Hoelzel

Helle Juul

Karla Kowalski

Anupama Kundoo

Anne Lacaton

Regine Leibinger

Lu Wenyu

Dorte Mandrup

Rozana Montiel

Kathrin Moore

Farshid Moussavi

Carme Pinós

Nili Portugali

Paula Santos

Kazuyo Sejima

Annabelle Selldorf

Pavitra Sriprakash

Siv Helene Stangeland

Brigitte Sunder-Plassmann

Lene Tranberg

Billie Tsien

Elisa Valero

Nathalie de Vries

Andrea Wandel

Helena Weber

Mona Bayr

Studio H₂A, Eislingen
Villa on Lake Constance, Germany, 2018

A courtyard house and a house by the lake: this building on Lake Constance presents two faces. The direct lakeside location and a desire to make the water visible and tangible as a moving element were a strong source of inspiration during the planning process. The basic form of the white building is a right-angled cube. The use of a lot of glass lends the building an airy and bright appearance as well as a certain lightness. The geometry of the building tells a story, every geometric feature having a functional and/or energy-related idea behind it.

The new ground and upper floor were added to the existing building, of which the basement and indoor pool were retained. Converted into an open-air swimming pool, the former indoor pool is now an eye-catcher on the north terrace, while the basement provides utility space. In contrast to the white, rather cool building front, a warm and elegant wooden finish was chosen for the quiet areas of the energy-efficient house. The east wing is thus completely clad with wood. Inside, wood-paneled elements can also be found, creating a perfect fusion of the individual parts of the building.

The geometry of the building lends it the appearance of two airy boxes balanced one on top of the other. The upper floor rests on the east and west wings and seems to float. Large shadow gaps between the east and west wings accentuate this effect. The design makes for a spacious living area on the ground floor, which connects through its glazed facade the terrace on the south side, with its view of the lake, to the courtyard and swimming pool on the north side. Like a sculptural object, the wood-clad sauna adheres to the cube on the upper floor and enjoys an unobstructed view of the lake.

With a total of 140 square meters the exterior facade of the building is almost entirely made of glass. Due to the narrow frames of the large sliding windows, it has been possible to create a seemingly continuous glass surface. In addition, the glass elements are not positioned directly at the edge of the building, but rather slightly indented, allowing the lake to be observed from as many angles as possible. The generous glass facades provide a direct view of Lake Constance. You can literally look through the house and, in doing so, perceive architectural elements inside that highlight this unique environment.

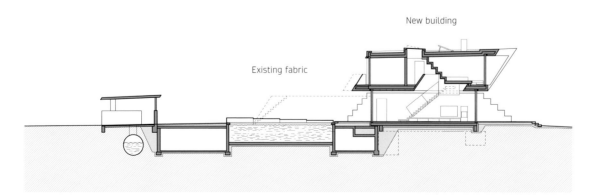

New building

Existing fabric

Cross section

The courtyard house
The facade facing the courtyard encloses the existing swimming pool and protects the courtyard from strong lake winds.

The house by the lake
There is an unobstructed view of Lake Constance from almost anywhere in the house.

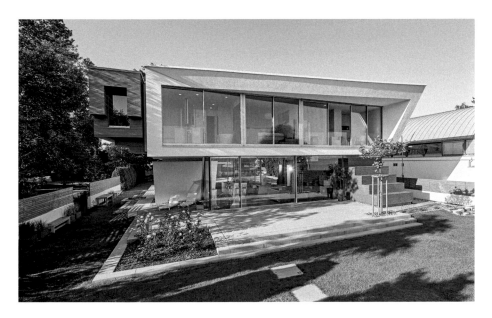

View from the gallery to the living
area on the first floor

Floor plan, second floor

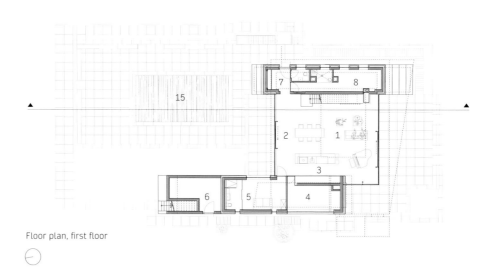

Floor plan, first floor

1 Living room	6 Garden house	11 Sauna
2 Dining room 1	7 Wardrobe	12 Rooms
3 Kitchen	8 Utility room	13 Bedroom
4 Dining room 2	9 Office	14 Cabinet space
5 Guest room	10 Toilet/bathroom	15 Pool

Odile Decq

Studio Odile Decq, Paris, France
Fangshan Tangshan National Geopark Museum, Nanjing, China, 2015

The Fangshan Tangshan National Geopark Museum was inscribed in a general scheme for the development of this important archaeological site. It was here in 1993 that the 600,000 year-old male and female skulls of *Homo erectus nankinensis* were discovered.

The shape of the museum finds its origin in the topography of the site. The natural contours were reinterpreted in volume to direct the lines of the building, which rises out of the ground in continuous bands around a large plaza. A specific aim of the project was that neither the building nor the site assume a dominant role. The continuity between the landscape and the museum creates a sequential museological space that runs through the many layers of the project, the floors seeming to imitate the Earth's crust. The "promenade" of discovery also follows the play of curved lines and the interaction between site and museum. From the outside, the museum is clearly perceptible through the glass facades in between the different layers of curved lines. A layer of horizontal stone elements placed in front of the facade

protects the glass and shields the interior from the sun. Colorful volumes are located on the ground floor, such as the main theater, a 4D cinema as well as a restaurant, café, and gift shops.

In museographical terms, the museum forms the encounter between geology and paleontology: the inner succession of museographic displays is the translation of this geological revelation. Entering the main hall, the shifted central void reveals the different layers throughout different floors. The museum's "promenade" of discovery offers the possibility of interaction that follow different museographic scales, allowing people to plan their visit efficiently based on the amount of time they want to spend at the museum. Each museum floor is widely open to the main facade which lets in an abundance of natural light, whereas the back of the museum, fitted into the side of the slope, is composed as a structural backbone that includes technical services, lifts, and emergency exits.

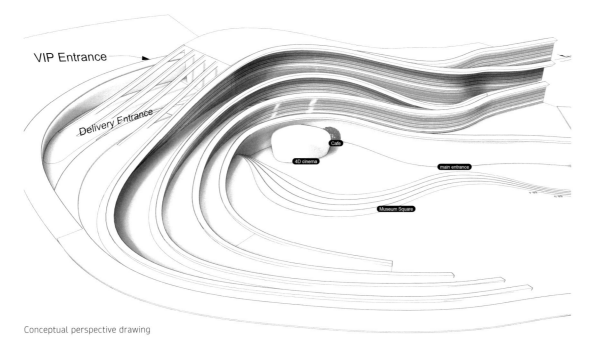

VIP Entrance

Delivery Entrance

Cafe

4D cinema

main entrance

Museum Square

Conceptual perspective drawing

The museum's floor lines resemble layers of a geological formation, giving it the appearance of having grown out of the landscape. It is located near the site of *Homo erectus nankinensis,* which is the starting point for the archaeological and geological exhibitions of the museum. The site is scenically linked to other attractions, including hot springs, a restaurant by the lake, and an information center for gold prospecting.

In the central, light-flooded atrium, the different floors of the museum and their flowing lines become visible. The exhibitions are designed in such a way that the visitor moves from top to bottom and reaches the next floor via the suspended staircase of the atrium.

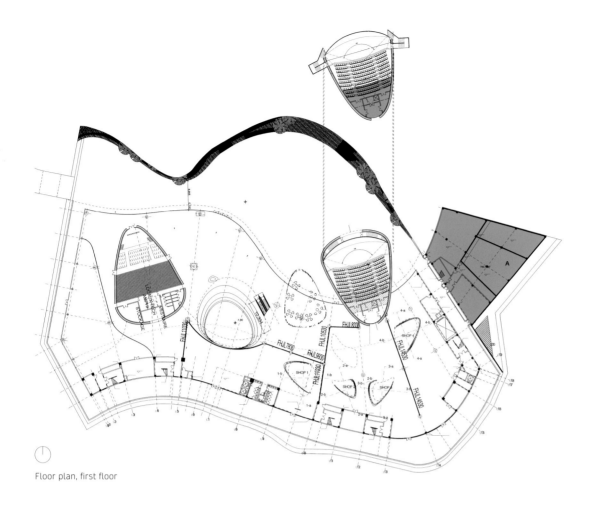

Floor plan, first floor

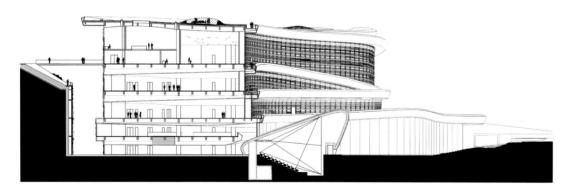

Cross section

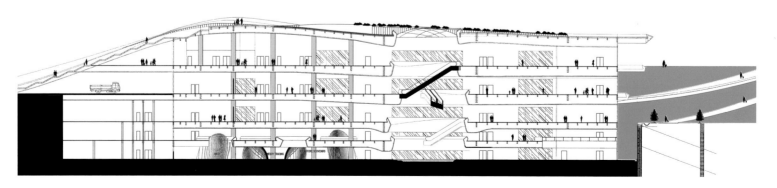

Longitudinal section

Elke Delugan-Meissl

Delugan Meissl Associated Architects, Vienna, Austria
Walkerhill Spa & Resort, Seoul, South Korea, since 2017

The Walkerhill is characterized by its irregular and hilly topography which affords many different and interesting views. The starting point of the project entailed finding a direct relation to the natural landscape. The building skin follows the flowing lines created by the existing topography. At the same time, these natural lines are powerfully punctuated with an infinity pool, terraces, and lounge areas. The building grows vertically towards the hillside, thus allowing the neighboring buildings to look over the new resort, with its pool and spa, without blocking their views.

Its envelope is a translucent skin, which allows a tenuous perception of the interior composition, the warm tones of the interior natural materials, the water reflections and the different functional areas. At the same time, the darker colors of the skin ensure privacy in the interior space. The project plays with the duality between introversion and exposure. On the one hand, it seeks contact with the surrounding setting by projecting some of its interior spaces and exterior pools out of the external building's shell. On the other hand, it offers intimacy and quietness.

The infinity pool is a spectacular eye-catcher, also visible from the outside since it cantilevers over the entrance area and towards the Han River. At 190 meters in length, the pool invites spa visitors to swim beyond the building boundary, creating a sensation of bathing in an elevated pool flying over the landscape below. On colder days, the pool can be heated like a gigantic public bathtub and during the wintertime, the pool can be transformed into a thrilling outdoor ice-skating area. The level below is designated for the exclusive use of special guests and offers a number of services, such as sports, places to relax, health treatments, and dining areas.

The rooftop has a generous lounge area, with lush greenery, art installations, and intimate relaxation areas with open fireplaces, thus offering a variety of venues, either for day-to-day use, or for staging special private or public events. The projection of this level towards the Han River, cantilevering out of the building shield, provides an ideal spot for visitors to savor the view.

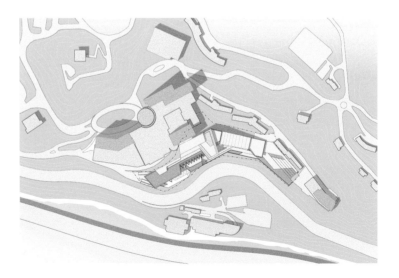

Site plan

The spa and wellness facility is located on a slope above the Han River. The building is developed from the site's topography, with various cantilevered elements, such as the infinity pool on the left, breaking through this contextual approach in an exciting way.

73

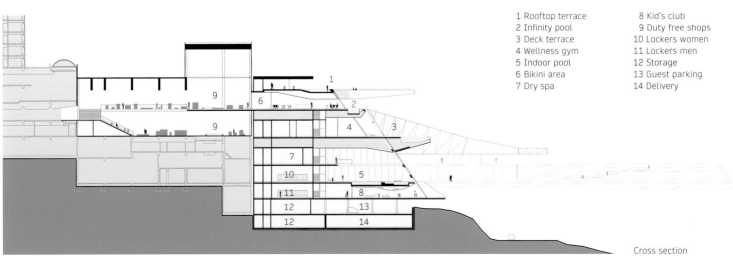

1 Rooftop terrace	8 Kid's club
2 Infinity pool	9 Duty free shops
3 Deck terrace	10 Lockers women
4 Wellness gym	11 Lockers men
5 Indoor pool	12 Storage
6 Bikini area	13 Guest parking
7 Dry spa	14 Delivery

Cross section

The indoor pool on the second floor has a glass facade along the side facing the river, thus offering an unobstructed view of the landscape.

Julie Eizenberg

Koning Eizenberg Architecture, Santa Monica, CA, US
Pico Branch Library, Santa Monica, CA, US, 2014

Community spaces are evolving to reach a public attracted to social energy and choice. Pico Neighborhood residents fought hard to have this public library located in a well-loved park and were invested participants in the public workshop that shaped its design. Conceived as a community living room, this branch library engages its park setting to encourage the use of an educational resource in a minority neighborhood. The project was developed with the community in a series of workshops which resulted in an inclusive design approach and interactive service strategies that attract families normally reticent to use institutional resources. It worked: in its first six months, the library lent 100,000 materials, welcomed 84,000 visitors, and registered 1,200 new borrowers.

The library is both a resource and social gathering place for a diverse community. Connections are key. Located in the center of Virginia Avenue Park, the library is surrounded by low income apartment residents to the north and single-family households to the south. The library's expressive identity and strategic plan moves activate formerly passive spaces to energize the setting. The front door opens to the weekend Farmers' Market, the community room amphitheater engages the Park Center program offerings, and the reading room provides a great view of pickup basketball games.

Visibility inside and out of the reading room is maximized by expansive shaded glass combined with large skylights. Oversized north-facing skylights amplify the light inside and reduce obscuring reflection from the outside. This integrated design approach to sustainability and daylight harvesting generated the architectural identity of the building and contributes to its LEED Platinum designation. If the library building

serves as an urban unifier, the roof structure is the unifying architectural form, it is also geared for performance, providing the surface area for a significant, LEED-platinum-worthy rainwater catchment system. The depth also accommodates the interior return air plenum.

The rectangular building sits at the site's center, oriented to harness optimal daylight. The library's community room—for meetings and after-school study programs—is located under the same roof structure but is detached and pulled to the other side of the mandatory fire truck lane that bisects the site south from Pico Boulevard to the north parking lot. The two volumes sit apart but remain connected by the steel framed canopy that serves as a support for photovoltaic panels, which together create an ornamental shadow pattern highlighting this north-south neighborhood path.

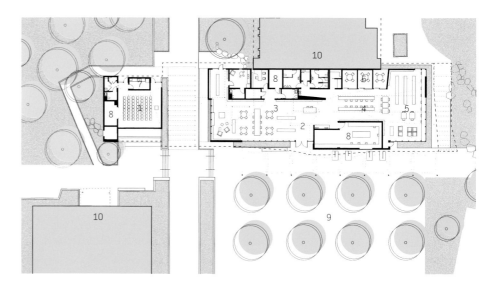

Site plan

1 Community room
2 Entry/checkout
3 Children's library
4 Computer Commons
5 Lounge
6 Group study room
7 Kitchen
8 Staff/support
9 Farmers' Market
10 Existing building

Reading room with cantilevered roof folded
into an ascending and descending landscape. The library building was developed in
a series of public design workshops together
with the residents of the neighborhood.

To the west is the community room, which
is connected to the library building via
a roof equipped with photovoltaics. The
steps in front of the building form an
outdoor meeting point.

The glass facade of the lounge provides
a view of the adjacent sports field.
The bright, cantilevered roof protects
the premises from direct sun.

The participatory planning process led
to the decision to preserve as much of
the park where the new library was to be
located as possible. The spatial link to the
Farmers' Market, which is held regularly
on the large, tree-planted square, was
also developed.

Manuelle Gautrand

Manuelle Gautrand Architecture, Paris, France
Alésia Cinema, Paris, France, 2016

The Alésia cinema is located on a main road in the south of Paris. Built entirely of reinforced concrete in the nineteen-twenties, it originally consisted of a single auditorium with 2,800 seats. Over the years it underwent several renovations until, in 2011, it was decided to completely rejuvenate the cinema.

The new building boasts the latest technology. It is approximately twenty-one meters higher than the former building and now houses six small and two large cinemas. The preservation of the exterior walls posed a challenge in terms of acoustics. The number of load-bearing construction points was kept to a minimum, and the insulation design chosen is self-supporting. The three-floor atrium behind the facade provides access to the cinema halls and open spaces. The ascending rows of seats form the step-like ceilings of the lobby. Small amphitheaters in front of the auditorium entrances provide space for informal gatherings or projections. The main entrance leads into a large hall, which is also a passageway to the Rue d'Alésia, after which the cinema is named, and along which a second new facade was built. The box office, seating areas, and a café are located in the foyer, which has a light and airy ambience. From there, escalators, stairs, and walkways lead to the cinema halls.

Ample consideration was given to achieving an architecture of light. The decisive idea was to digitally animate the facade around the clock. A 500-square-meter media curtain was thus installed, constantly projecting moving images into the street. The facade is divided into twelve multi-folded bands. The bands

in the center of the facade are made of glass and covered with LED modules. At the edges bordering on the neighboring buildings, they are made of metal and also folded several times. The individual bands can show different pictures or film clips independently of each other or together to create a single image. The glass elements, fixed on steel frames, bend backwards towards the edge of the roof to form the roof construction. Lower down the facade, the bands tilt horizontally and form a cantilevered canopy of roughly three meters, also covered with LED modules. From there, film sequences can be projected directly onto the pavement, giving the audience the feeling of entering the cinema through a screen. The transparency of the facade, especially at night, creates the impression of a picture in space. A darker projection on the facade allows a free view inside to the lower part of the cinema halls and the open atrium. A brighter image reveals the folds of the facade.

Like an art installation with moving poetic images that are characteristic of motion pictures, the architecture mirrors the inner life of the cinema.

Longitudinal section through the foyer, which is open over all floors, and the movie theaters on all levels.

The conversion and modernization of the Alésia cinema in the Montparnasse district, which originally dates from the nineteen-twenties, includes as its most impressive change the installation of a media facade on which films can be advertised on a large scale.

Fourteen vertical strips of glass equipped with LED modules cover the facade in a pleated form, thus lending it depth. These pleats continue in steel and without LEDs towards the neighboring buildings, thus cleverly hiding the fire escape and technical facilities.

Opposite
In the foyer, the different floors are connected via air spaces. The ascending rows of seats in the cinemas became the motif for the top and bottom views of the stairs, which function as tiered seating areas.

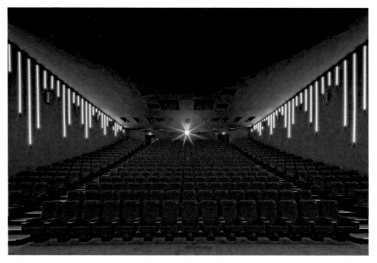

One of the eight movie theaters on the fourth floor

Annette Gigon

Annette Gigon/Mike Guyer Architekten, Zurich, Switzerland
Würth Haus Rorschach, Rorschach, Switzerland, 2013

Located by Lake Constance, Würth Haus Rorschach is a greenish glass structure that oscillates between transparency and reflection. Mirroring the distinctive features of the surrounding environment in many ways, the structured volume of the building responds to the nearby train station with lower cubes and to the vastness of the nearby park and lake with a higher volume. Maple trees characterize and enliven the space. A wide canopy enhances the main entrance. Visitors enter the building through a high entrance hall, which gives way to various walkways.

The business premises of the Würth Group, the training and conference rooms, the congress hall, and the restaurant are grouped around a spacious foyer with a central atrium and are connected to each other by an extensive staircase. Both the congress center with accommodation for five hundred people in the west and the public exhibition rooms of the Forum Würth in the southern part of the building have their own direct access and can therefore be used independently of the rest of the building.

Visitors to Forum Würth are guided through a reception area and museum shop to two differently sized, centrally lit exhibition rooms on the first floor. The shed skylight construction in the exhibition rooms also supports the cantilever of the canopy. Offices are located on four floors in the highest part of the building, which is not open to the public. Meeting areas with balconies face the lake; transparent or closed meeting rooms and offices alternate with open office space.

A glass shell covers the entire building complex. This outer, rear-ventilated glass layer is formed by staggered, slightly tinted glass panels that have a fine, metallic, shiny fabric inlay. This results in a rhythmic glass "curtain" that not only protects the building from sea winds and street noise, but also from heat or cold. The inner skin consists of triple insulating panes and thermal insulation with sheet metal cladding. The glass structure continues on the roof in the form of photovoltaic panels and green glass shards made of recycled glass.

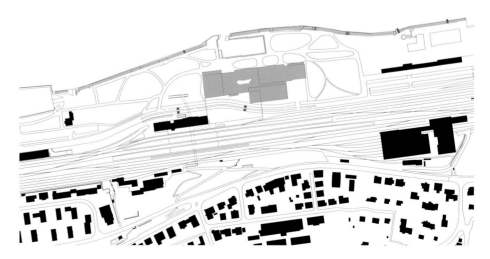

Site plan

The glass building reacts to its
surroundings with varying building
volumes. On the side facing the station,
the cubes are slightly lower than on
the lake side and a projecting canopy
roof points to the entrance.

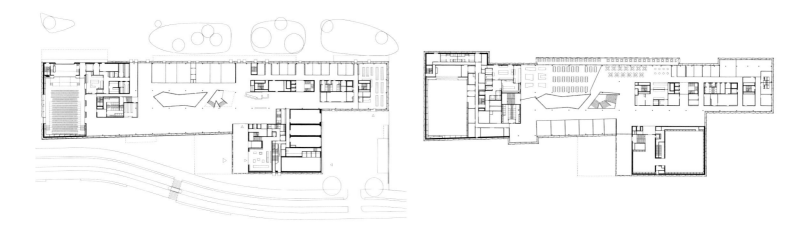

Floor plan, first floor

Floor plan, second floor

Opposite, bottom
The surrounding glass facade consists of
two layers: the outer, rear-ventilated layer
is composed of staggered, slightly greenish
glass panes with a shiny metallic fabric
inlay. The resulting rhythmic glass "curtain"
is intended to protect the building not only
from the lake winds and street noise, but
also from heat input and cooling.

Bottom
The publicly accessible areas are
arranged around an atrium.

Silvia Gmür

Silvia Gmür Reto Gmür Architekten, Basel, Switzerland
Bürgerspital Solothurn, Solothurn, Switzerland, since 2013

The facade of a building is a shell as well as a boundary. It is solid or permeable, repellent or communicative. The structure's identity is expressed by its facade and windows. The different uses of a building require different designs for the facade filter. The quality of the interior depends on the quality of the windows. Materiality and technology are thus transformed into sensory perception.

The new building project of the Solothurn public hospital is the result of an international tender for a hospital with 290 beds as well as for all the necessary examination and treatment wards and departments of an acute-care hospital on the site of the old hospital. The old hospital was to continue normal operation during the construction period. The design envisaged two new buildings arranged in an L-shape, to be built around the existing building. After completion of the new complex, a spacious park is to replace the old buildings, with the new hospital aligned with the park.

The two-story high base construction, in which the examination and treatment areas as well as the public space are located, strictly separates the access areas from the hospital care areas; it is linear, variable, and expandable. The main part of this area includes the wards on one side and the offices for staff, and storage space for beds and material on the other. Access areas along the facades open onto resting and exercise zones. By relocating the infrastructural components to the peripheral zones of the building, a main functional area will be created in a "columned hall." An open area of approximately 8,500 square meters per floor thus provides the greatest possible freedom for the organization of the individual medical departments.

The facade of the upper ward section emulates the closer rhythm of the patient rooms. It is characterized by a 1.4-meter-deep spatial layer, thereby creating the necessary distance between inside and outside, private and public areas. It provides visual protection

from the outside and an extension into the landscape from the inside. The external sun protection elements allow sufficient daylight while protecting the patient's room from heat and glare. The sun protection elements are prefabricated as hollow structures in order to minimize the loads. They are made of fiber-reinforced concrete with a maximum material thickness of three centimeters and suspended floor-by-floor from a stainless steel substructure.

Light plays a special role in the expression of the facade and in this project in general; it is considered a health-promoting factor in hospital construction, both inside and out.

The design consists of a new, L-shaped building arranged as a flat basement around the existing tower house. The facades are designed as a light-filtering layer, thus creating a transition zone between the intimate hospital rooms and the public exterior.

Site plan

View into one of the inner courtyards of the low building. The facade provides protection from view and direct sunlight, thus taking on not only a separating function, but also regulating the climate on the inside.

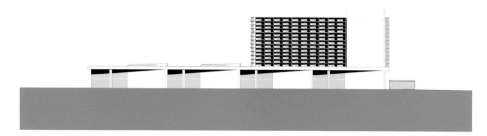

Elevation

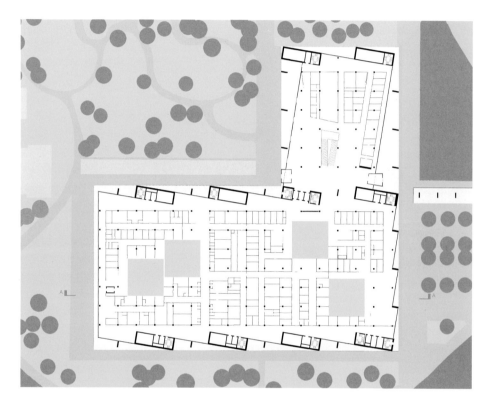

Floor plan

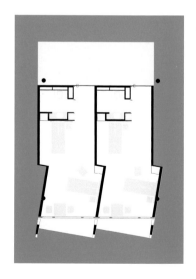

Floor plan, room for two patients. By offsetting and inclining the walls, individual, private areas are created for the patients.

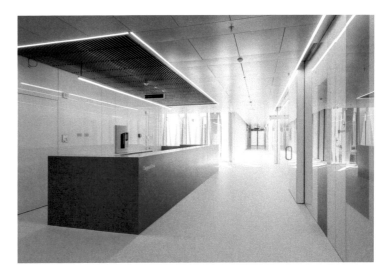

The reception area of the day clinic
is supplied with daylight via one of the
inner courtyards.

Cristina Guedes

Menos é Mais Architectos, Porto, Portugal
Arquipélago—Center for Contemporary Art, Ribeira Grande,
Azores, Portugal, 2014

In recent years, industrial structural change has often led to redundant factories being converted into cultural institutions. This is the case in Ribeira Grande on São Miguel, the main island of the Azores archipelago in the Atlantic Ocean. There, a former tobacco and spirits factory has been converted into an art and cultural center.

Instead of demolishing the partially derelict existing buildings, they were integrated into the overall architectural concept. The design does not attempt to emphasize the differences between the old and new buildings; on the contrary, it seeks to unite the different scales and historical epochs of its components. The existing buildings are characterized by volcanic stone masonry, which has been preserved and extensively renovated. The new one-story and two-story complex concrete structure display abstract form, without reference.

The Arquipélago—Center for Contemporary Art now offers exhibition space and a multi-purpose hall, library, workshops and studios, as well as offices, a cafeteria, a shop, and storage space on more than 9,000 square meters. The two-story building to the west has a basement and houses the auditorium and workshops, while the building opposite to the east houses the entrance and foyer, offices, and utility rooms. The larger old building contains the exhibition halls, which are up to 4.5 meters high; the smaller industrial buildings with their gabled roofs contain twenty-four workrooms.

The new concrete buildings are positioned in such a way that two connected inner courtyards were created with the existing buildings, opening up the boundaries between public and private space, art and life. Basalt stone from the volcanic island of São Miguel has been used for the floor.

While the two-story existing exhibition building is white both on the inside and outside and is furnished with light wooden floors and stairs, the new buildings are completely black. Their facades are made of dark exposed concrete. The height and the sloping roof are adapted to the existing building. Local basalt aggregates and iron oxide pigments provide the almost black color. The uneven surface emulates the coarse stone facades of the existing buildings. To provide a contrast to the dark textures, a few golden color accents, such as a railing or a deeply set window soffit, have been included. Daylight only enters through narrow ground level windows. The entrance to the new building faces the street and has been cut into the sloping wall as a narrow slit.

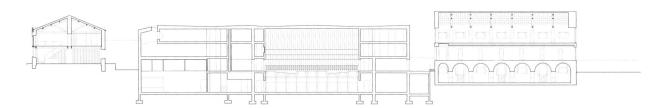

Sectional view through the existing building (left and right) and the new multifunctional hall (center)

The former factory, which was originally used for tobacco and then alcohol production, had been empty for about fifty years. Repurposing the building for cultural use as a place of artistic production and exhibition was intended to revitalize the site and save its existence.

Bottom
Two new buildings were added to the eight existing buildings in such a way that a complex was created which, like a small town, connects multiple squares via alleys. At the public entrance plaza, the existing white building is excitingly juxtaposed with the new dark-gray building.

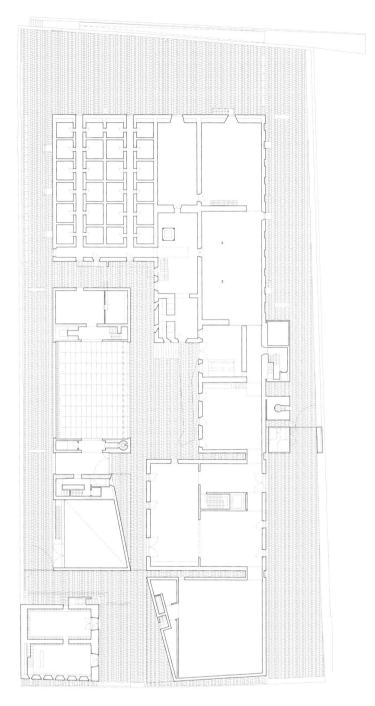

Floor plan, first floor

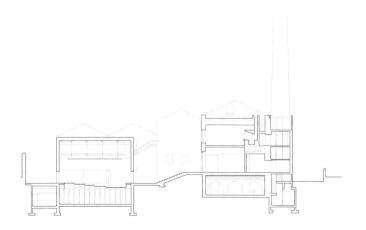

Sectional view through the new multi-functional hall (left) and workshops and rehearsal rooms in an existing building (right)

The central courtyard connects the multi-functional hall on the left with the workshops and rehearsal rooms on the right in the existing buildings. The dark gray of the exposed concrete was achieved with volcanic aggregates.

Right
The striking silhouette of the former factory buildings facing the sea has been preserved.

Melkan Gürsel

Tabanlıoğlu Architects, Istanbul, Turkey
Dakar Congress Center, Dakar, Senegal, 2014

Dakar, the capital city of Senegal, is located at the westernmost tip of the country on the Cap-Vert peninsula. The area's local geography and natural values were the inspiration for the Dakar Congress Center project. One of Senegal's extraordinary landmark features includes Baobabs. These distinctive trees, with their enormous girth, live well over a thousand years. Many of them have been classified as historic trees by the Ministry of Culture.

Dakar Congress Center's surrounding water element and the "girth" of the project refer to resource values. Longevity is the aim, both for the physical existence of the building and the power of the country, and also that the Center be a source of pride for Africa. Sheltered as if by an ancient, monumental tree, the one-piece roof of the project encases the building stacks, and protects them against weather conditions, such as direct sun or wind. The units of the complex are connected across the surrounding water by bridges, which emphasizes notions of the community's foundation-creation, duration-continuity, and harmony-order, in both social and environmental realms.

The rectangular blocks are nested in a semi-transparent metal envelope, which acts as a shield protecting the interiors from excessive sun, ensuring they benefit from optimum daylight. A mesh curtain flows around the building, screening the inner glass walls and reducing the heat in order to improve the building's energy efficiency.

The three-dimensional effect of the curtain gives the building the impression of floating over the surrounding reflection pool. The presidential entrance leads through the main lobby to the main conference hall, which can seat 1,500 delegates. The public entrances on the west side access the public restaurant, the open-air fair zone, and the adjacent press and administration building. The VIP entrance is at the east end of the complex, between the museum unit and the VIP unit, which is linked to the main hall via a transparent connection bridge. The upper level is reserved exclusively for the President of Senegal.

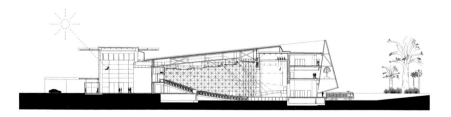

Cross section

Like a baobab tree, a large roof spans
the entire complex of the congress center.
The tree, which can live up to 1,000 years,
is an important element in Senegalese
cultural heritage.

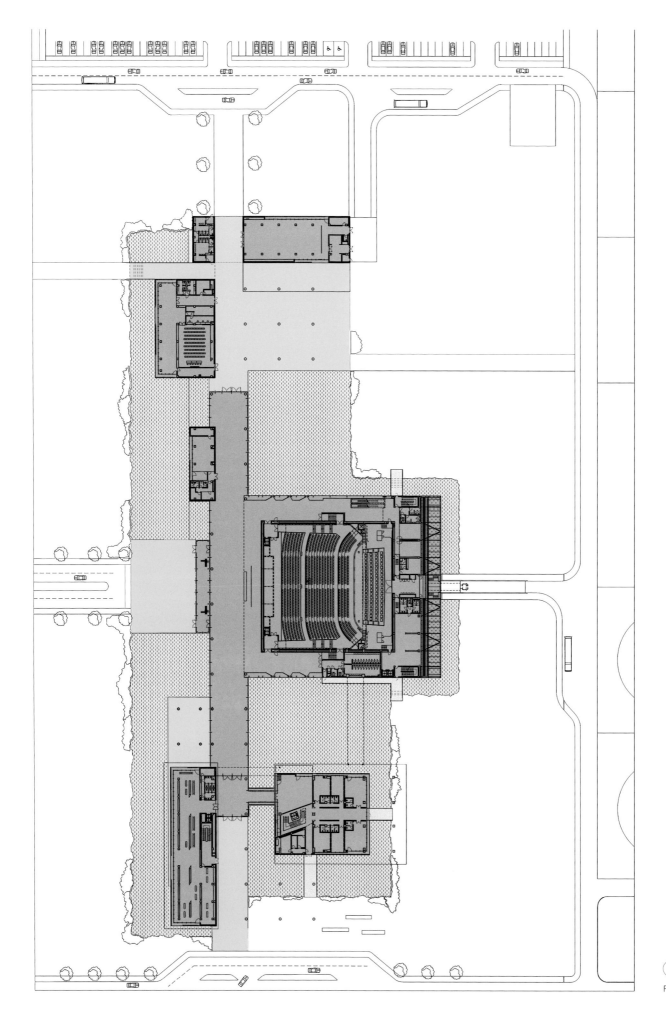

Floor plan

The entire complex is surrounded by water basins that reflect the different colors of the cubes, wrapped in translucent metal, and connecting bridges.

Itsuko Hasegawa

Itsuko Hasegawa Atelier, Tokyo, Japan
Suzu City Performing Arts Center, Suzu, Japan, 2006

Suzu is blessed with natural beauty. The city also hands down traditions through festivals held in each district. The bamboo flutes used in the Kiriko festival, one of Noto Peninsula's foremost festivals, differ subtly in melody and tone in each district, and this sound tradition, too, is actively being handed down in Suzu. During our workshops, many residents voiced a desire for a hall with good acoustics. But there were also many people who expressed a desire for a venue offering theater, dance, and movies. We therefore designed a concert hall with movable sound reflector boards, enabling it to be used as a multipurpose hall. We established 942-millimeter-diameter diatomite plates on the wall in a Mameshibori pattern (traditional spotted pattern) to serve as sound reflectors, with a glass fiber filling the intervals as sound absorbing material.

Suzu is said to have the world's largest deposits of diatomaceous earth. Asked by the city administration to employ diatomaceous earth, I researched its potential as an acoustic material and discovered that it softly reflects sound when applied to walls in a plaster. Later, when actually listening, we found that the walls impart richness and warmth to the sound from everything from traditional *shamisen* and *koto* to modern orchestras. I also employed diatomaceous earth in the walls of the small rooms and in the wall embedded with small stainless mirrors in the lobby, as well as in the ground surface of the exterior sound plaza.

I have continually proposed "landscape architecture," believing that public space should be like a *harappa* (open field). This building in Suzu accordingly maintains integrity between inside and outside. When creating event spaces for picnics and traditional arts outside the building, I focused on a green environment, bringing it inside the building by flooring the lobby with a carpet bearing a lawn-grass pattern.

I also wanted the Center to help respond to the needs of Suzu's aging society. As a keyword for this, I arrived at the expression *kyosei* (together—exist), meaning to live together.

My inspiration? Looking down at Suzu from the airplane, I saw a beautiful, poetic landscape of clouds floating like round pillows. This image remained in my mind. Standing before the children of the remote, seaside city, I held my first workshop. "What kind of building will you design?" they asked. "A building like clouds in the sky," I replied. My image was conveyed to everyone and shared, and the building was born in its present form. Twenty-four big and small round clouds, as if floating in from the ocean, congregate to form a large roof under which people can gather and enjoy culture.

Itsuko Hasegawa

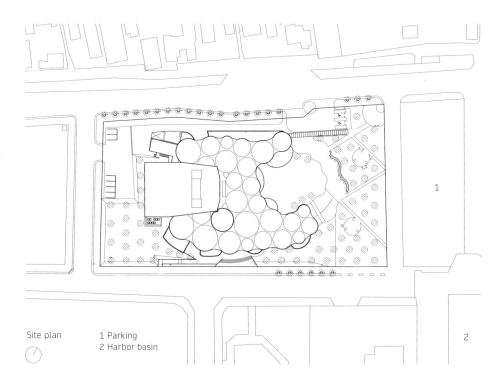

Site plan   1 Parking
                2 Harbor basin

The cultural center is designed as an architecture of the landscape. Like clouds, a gently undulating and curved structure covers the complex, which opens up to a wide lawn.

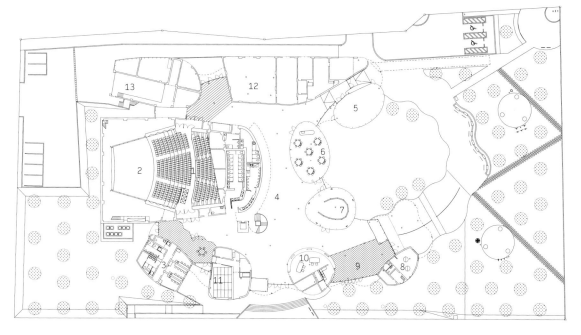

1 Hall
2 Stage
3 Dressing room
4 Lobby
5 Civic salon
6 Workshop
7 Flute museum
8 Kids' room
9 Café
10 Office
11 Tatami room
12 Machine room
13 Delivery entrance

Floor plan, first floor

View into the perforated aluminum cladding of the ceilings; in the background, the harbor zone and the sea.

Opposite, top
Transparency and reflections of the glass facades allow interior and exterior space to merge..

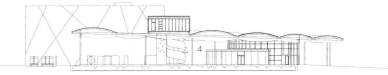

Cross section

Anna Heringer (left) and Dominique Gauzin-Müller

Anna Heringer

Studio Anna Heringer, Laufen, Germany
Bamboo Hostel, Baoxi, China, 2016

Our physically limited planet is inhabited by a fast-growing population endangered by global warming. The construction industry plays an important role in this environmental crisis: it consumes about 40 percent of resources and is responsible for 40 percent of the waste production and anthropogenic greenhouse gases. Cement manufacturing produces alone about 7 percent of CO_2 emissions. It is time to decrease drastically the grey energy of buildings. Earth and bio-based materials, which require very little energy for their transformation, are available nearly everywhere and using them creatively contributes to the much needed ecological and social transition.

Since resources are becoming increasingly scarce, the architecture of tomorrow must become frugal as regards ground, energy, and materials. This simplicity that concentrates on real needs can still produce happy and satisfying results. Anna Heringer proved it in 2005 with her diploma project, the METI School in Rudrapur. This project, which she worked on with Eike Roswag, won the 2007 Aga Khan Award for Architecture and many other prizes. This "handmade school," built for and with the inhabitants of a village in Bangladesh, changed the image of earth and bamboo architecture. The universal beauty of this building has inspired thousands of professionals and students, promoting the development of design-build projects in many universities. Each building designed by Anna Heringer emerges from the *genius loci*, fits in the regional ecosystem and finds a balance between the wisdom of vernacular construction and the comfort of modernity.

The guesthouse complex erected in 2016 in Baoxi, China, showcases it in a wonderful way. It participated in the First International Bamboo Architecture Biennale, which took place in the region of Longquan, for which twelve well-known architects (including Simon Velez and Kengo Kuma) were invited to build permanent bamboo structures. The hostels, inspired by Chinese lampshades, shine in the night. Their core,

made of rammed earth on a pebble masonry base, is enveloped in an expressive woven bamboo structure. The three buildings celebrate the beauty of natural materials and show that they can be used in a contemporary way, unlike many traditional houses that conceal their earth walls behind fake facades.

With this project, Anna Heringer wanted "to reconnect with cultural goods shaped out of immanent material characteristics, like the bending strength of bamboo, and with the rich handicraft tradition of China like basket weaving. The applied techniques are labor intensive, challenge the skills of local craftsmen and leave the biggest part of the profit to the community." In Europe, as well as in Africa and Asia, the young German architect favors non-standardized local materials "because they lead to more diversity in cities and rural regions, foster fair economics through job creation and preserve our planet's ecosystem."

Anna Heringer's work shows, in a convincing way, that a building can be simple, meaningful, and beautiful and that "a strong 'charming power' lies in the authenticity of natural materials." According to this socially engaged woman, "architecture is a tool to improve life."

Dominique Gauzin-Müller

The Bamboo Hostels were created as part of the First International Bamboo Architecture Biennale in Baoxi. The region is known for its craft traditions in bamboo processing and ceramics. The white cantilevered bodies behind the bamboo cover are "sleeping cocoons," each offering space for two guests.

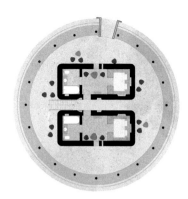
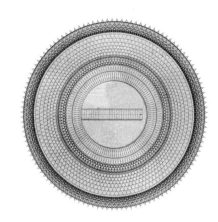

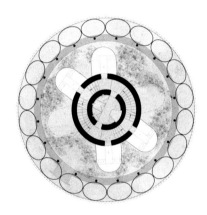

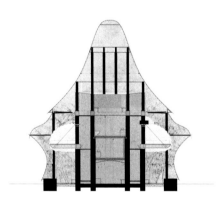

Section, ground plan and top view (from left to right) of the three round buildings "Nightingale," "Peacock" and "Dragon." Each building has a massive cylinder made of rammed earth, which contains access and sanitary rooms.

The shells of the hostels, inspired by traditional Chinese lampshades, consist of a coarse-meshed weave of fine bamboo sticks, the substructure of which is composed of steel rings and bamboo supports.

Right
Construction of the building core made of rammed earth over pebble masonry.

Fabienne Hoelzel

Fabulous Urban, Zurich, Switzerland
Makoko Neighborhood Hotspot, Lagos, Nigeria, 2017

Fabulous Urban developed and implemented the Makoko Neighborhood Hotspot as part of the Makoko Urban Design Toolbox and the Makoko/Iwaya Waterfront Regeneration Plan. The Makoko Neighborhood Hotspot was designed as a technical and social infrastructure for Makoko, one of Lagos's best-known urban slum settlements. It serves as an infrastructure hub providing urban services such as biogas-linked community toilets and as a business incubator promoting waste-to-energy principles. Its purpose is to serve at large as a community empowerment tool and learning center.

The Hotspot represents more of a concept than a project even though the architectural design aspect was carefully and ambitiously developed. Its conceptualization and building phases confronted the poor underserved Makoko communities with a series of tough and difficult decision-making processes. After the completion of the structure and its inauguration in December 2015, the second project phase led in 2016 to the formation of the Makoko Neighborhood Hotspot Multipurpose Cooperative Society Limited, officially registered at the Lagos State Department of Cooperatives. It serves as the operational and administrative body of the Hotspot.

One of the key tasks of the committee is the hiring, payment, and supervision of employees. For this purpose, three business plans were drafted to ensure the sustainable set-up and long-term operation of the envisioned Hotspot activities. Since December 2017, the end of the third project phase, the implemented business activities—biogas-linked community toilets, biogas production, water treatment, and farming pipes—have provided the badly needed infrastructure for roughly 200 people.

As a business incubator, the Hotspot serves as a pilot or prototype approach that could and should be replicated in other parts of the community and in other low-income settlements in Lagos State. One of the long-term goals of the Neighborhood Hotspot initiative is to inspire government officials by showing them how the dramatic lack of infrastructure in many communities and within large parts of the population could be approached, namely with such decentralized, strategic yet low-cost interventions.

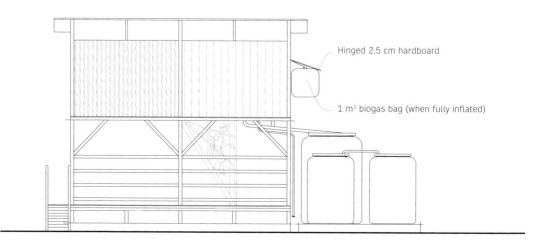

Hinged 2.5 cm hardboard

1 m³ biogas bag (when fully inflated)

Elevation

The Makoko Hotspot is a prototype of a decentralized neighborhood center in a fishermen's settlement in Nigeria that is intended to help establish local organizational structures in the form of a cooperative. The core business of the cooperative is the production of biogas from waste.

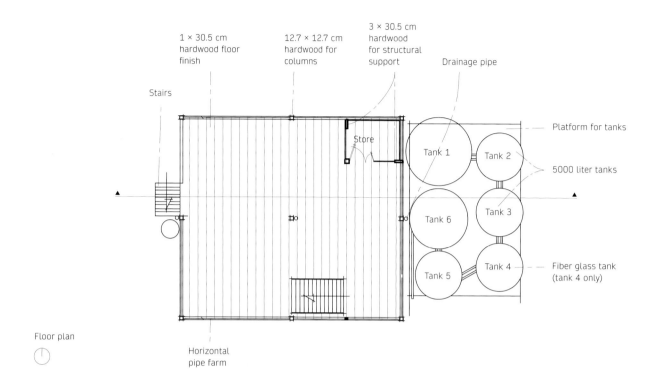

1 × 30.5 cm hardwood floor finish

12.7 × 12.7 cm hardwood for columns

3 × 30.5 cm hardwood for structural support

Drainage pipe

Stairs

Store

Platform for tanks

Tank 1

Tank 2

5000 liter tanks

Tank 6

Tank 3

Tank 5

Tank 4

Fiber glass tank (tank 4 only)

Floor plan

Horizontal pipe farm

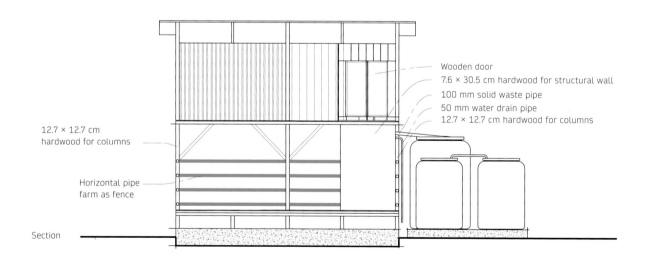

12.7 × 12.7 cm hardwood for columns

Horizontal pipe farm as fence

Wooden door
7.6 × 30.5 cm hardwood for structural wall
100 mm solid waste pipe
50 mm water drain pipe
12.7 × 12.7 cm hardwood for columns

Section

In addition to biogas production,
rainwater is also collected, filtered,
and stored in large blue cannisters that
can be accessed by local residents.

Right
The Hotspot is not only a business
incubator, but also the social center
of the neighborhood.

Helle Juul

Juul Frost Arkitekter, Copenhagen, Denmark
Campus Örebro, Örebro, Sweden, 2017

A growing interdependency and a new set of shared values between universities, cities, and business communities is changing the concept and physical organization of campus areas. The city of Örebro is currently undergoing a development that will transform it into a Knowledge City—defined by the interconnectedness and collaborations between academia, the city, and its businesses.

The design of Örebro Campus was grounded in methods, tools, and a theoretical framework developed by Juul Frost Arkitekter through the research projects "The University of the Future" (2004) and "The Future Campus: from 'the Academic Village' to 'Urban University Hub'" (2007). The research projects outlined the categories of needs as social, functional, educational, and urban, in order to ensure holistic solutions. The project developed robust and adaptable tools to integrate the campus with the city which is to transform into a Knowledge City.

Three new buildings in relation to the Campus Square have been programmed and designed in detail, and thereby provided the university with a vibrant, urban, and inviting entrance area—an arrival point, that connects the campus with the city.

To integrate campus and city, plug-ins are used, a process which involves urban features being actively drawn into the campus area, just as, vice versa, campus features can be drawn into the city through plug-outs. Accordingly, Örebro Campus was conceived with student housing and accommodation for researchers, with a café and bookstore on the ground floor: urban functions that intensify the life in the new entrance area. Concrete discs displaced in the manner of ice floes form the Campus Square,

the new gathering point between Örebro University and the city. Narrow slits run through the square and open into larger fissures filled out with roughly hewn granite stones that conduct the rainwater towards the center of the square, a grove of white birch trees. In the new entrance area, the city's floor has been dragged into the building. The Campus Square breaches the NOVA house through large glass sections, opening the lower floor of the building in a transilluminated aula. Thus, the continued materiality dissolves the boundary between the business school's premises and the public space of the city, underpinning Örebro Campus's transformation from an "academic village" to a "university hub"—a campus that is not defined by its borders but the exchange with the city and its firms.

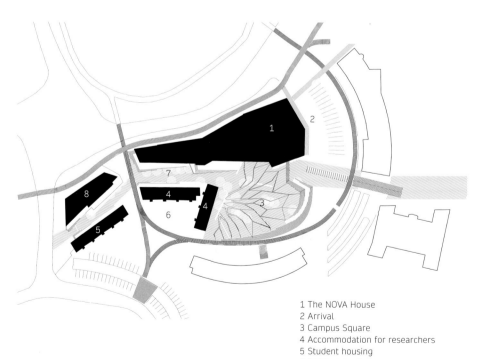

Site plan

1 The NOVA House
2 Arrival
3 Campus Square
4 Accommodation for researchers
5 Student housing
6 Campus garden
7 Campus street
8 Not realized

112

The heart of the campus is NOVA House, which connects the campus with the city providing a place of exchange. Open auditoriums like the one in the lower part of the entrance hall allow informal meetings.

View of the central square of the campus,
with NOVA House on the right and a
building with apartments for researchers.
Like a public arena, the tiered steps in
Campus Square are an ideal meeting
place.

In front of the research building, the square's paving stones give way to gravel, trees, and concrete slabs staggered like ice floes.

Karla Kowalski

Szyszkowitz-Kowalski + Partner, Graz, Austria
Sparkasse Courtyards, Graz, Austria, 2010

The city center of Graz, the European Capital of Culture in 2003, is remarkable for the expressiveness of its roofs and especially for its Italian-style Renaissance courtyards. In the crowded inner-city center, the project covers the entire premises of the Sparkasse bank, an area predestined for the construction of a sequence of three inner courtyards, stretching from the newly adapted bank grounds to the Andreas-Hofer-Platz development area. These three courtyards have a special character due to their specific architectural design.

With its inverted pyramid shape, the central courtyard provides a formative atmosphere for the entire complex. The other two courtyards were also created in keeping with the urban theme of courtyards predominant in Graz. This, in turn, suits the small-scale nature of the historical ensemble and creates a quarter that perfectly fits into the urban space of the city, despite its contemporary architectural language. The new components are thus intended to be an urban and architectural supplement to the historical buildings. On the sloping walls of the central courtyard, planted troughs are interspersed between two new, barrel-type vaulted wings, evoking the motif of hanging gardens. In addition, the intensive planting has created several green courtyards, functioning as a green lung for this part of the city, which used to be a closed and sealed area.

The cubature and contour of the courtyard finds expression in the facade of the building complex facing the public square, thus responding to the expressiveness of the historic old town. The theme of architectural facades opening upwards thus becomes an analogy to the inclined glass elements of this courtyard and in essence determines the entire design. This arrangement results in an optimal assessment of the natural lighting and ventilation of the office complex. This is in line with the client's wish to implement an energy concept based on geothermal drilling as well as pre-cooling and pre-warming of the building structures, displacement ventilation for the trapped outside space, and adjustable shading of the courtyard.

On the street side, the U-shaped bank building closes the block. The inner courtyard, which is concealed behind the building and opens upwards, is mirrored with glass louvers in the central section of the facade.

Floor plan, fifth floor

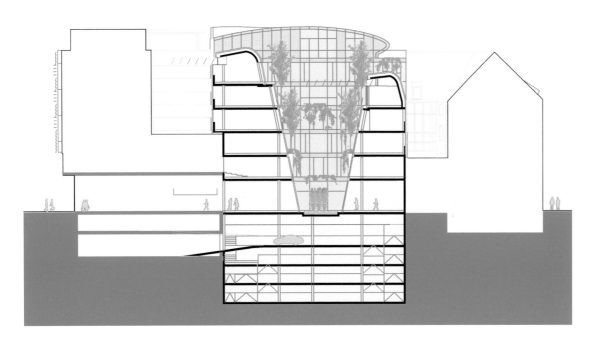

Cross section

View into the inner courtyard, which
is stepped down like an inverted pyramid
and is intended to transform the courtyard into a garden by means of white tree
troughs integrated into the facade. The
steel and glass construction of the facade
facilitates optimal light and sightlines.

Anupama Kundoo

Anupama Kundoo Architects, Auroville/Berlin, India/Germany
Full Fill Homes, Auroville, India, 2016

Housing in India needs to be produced with significantly fewer resources than globally accepted standards, given the huge population on comparatively much less land. Sustainable building approaches need to be affordable too. "Full Fill Homes" relies on structural ingenuity and engineering to achieve innovative high-speed, lightweight construction, saving materials, energy, and time. Prefabricated ferro-cement modules produced in homes of local masons can be assembled on site in six days, including the foundation. Folded forms give strength to thin elements creating cavities, which become the complete storage solution for the homeowners, making furniture redundant and rooms spacious. Bright happy colors accentuate and define the elements, in keeping with the aesthetic values of the local context.

Modest but high-quality spaces for individuals are supported by shared spaces of different degrees to create community and healthy interdependence. Common kitchen and laundry facilities liberate personal free time and space while sharing resources. Flexible modular prefabricated units allow user-participation and creative combinations. Healthy working conditions created in the backyards of masons' homes enable them to work from home instead of centralized factory conditions. This permits flexible timings, eases the participation of women, encourages small entrepreneurs, and builds knowledge and disseminates it naturally.

Ferro-cement technology is further optimized through significant reduction of easily available materials (chicken mesh replaces steel bars, mortar replaces concrete); reduction of high embodied energy, energy in production process and transport; avoidance of industrial finishing material; water-efficient fabrication and curing, and superior ductile properties against seismic forces that are an emerging concern due to climate change. Replacing chicken mesh with jute and

natural fibers is being investigated for future prototypes. The short assembly period further reduces the environmental footprint, being sensitive to existing flora, fauna, and neighbors.

Apart from making housing affordable and accessible, the project generates employment, builds knowledge and skills, and empowers local people and small entrepreneurs. Affordability is due to engineering efficiency and high-speed fabrication: it is easy to learn and users may participate in its construction to reduce costs further. These versatile elements can be dismantled in a day, reassembled in various configurations, or even shifted elsewhere. Furniture costs are saved too.

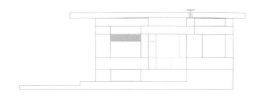

Elevation, side

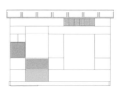

Elevation, front

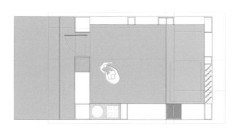

Floor plan

A prototype of the Full Fill Home, a modular system based on prefabricated box modules made of ferro-cement, was shown on a scale of 1:1 in the Arsenale during the 2016 Architecture Biennale in Venice.

After its dismantling in Chennai, the first
prototype of the Full Fill Home was rebuilt
in Auroville, India, where it has been used
as a design studio ever since.

The manufacturing process of the
ferro-cement modules, which are based
on vernacular manufacturing methods,
is easy to learn and takes less than
48 hours, followed by 3 to 4 weeks
curing time.

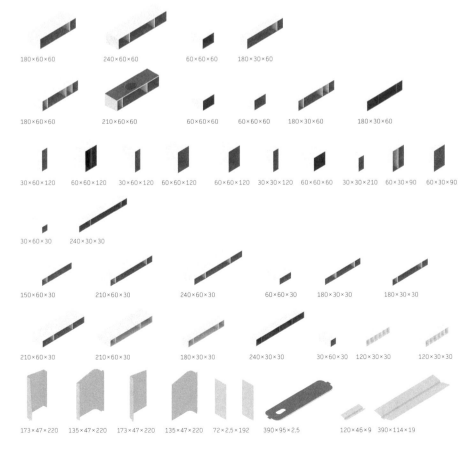

180×60×60	240×60×60	60×60×60	180×30×60

180×60×60	210×60×60	60×60×60	60×60×60	180×30×60	180×30×60

30×60×120	60×60×120	30×60×120	60×60×120	60×60×120	30×30×120	60×60×60	30×30×210	60×30×90	60×30×90

30×60×30	240×30×30

150×60×30	210×60×30	240×60×30	60×60×30	180×30×30	180×30×30

210×60×30	210×60×30	180×30×30	240×30×30	30×60×30	120×30×30	120×30×30

173×47×220	135×47×220	173×47×220	135×47×220	72×2,5×192	390×95×2,5	120×46×9	390×114×19

To make the thin, 25 cm ferro-cement elements stiffer, they are folded into rectangular boxes that can be used as storage space or seating.

Inventory of the ferro-cement modules required for the construction of a Full Fill Home and associated Easy-WC prototypes

Anne Lacaton (right) and Jean-Philippe Vassal

Anne Lacaton

Lacaton & Vassal Architectes, Montreuil, France
Housing Transformation, Saint-Nazaire, France, 2016

This twin operation of transformation and densification was implemented in La Chesnaie in Saint-Nazaire, an emblematic area in terms of nineteen-seventies town planning. It falls within the framework of the Ville-Ouest urban renewal project, through which the commune is continuing its development along the ring road between the city center and the town of Pornichet.

Ideally situated between sea and city center, this area, which has many things going for it—a green wooded site, beaches and open spaces for walking nearby, different amenities, quality housing, public transport—had nonetheless lost its appeal. Contrary to current urban policy, which wisely encourages the demolition of such areas regardless of their potential, the project proposed long-term rejuvenation through the radical transformation of forty apartments in one of the existing high-rises and its densification through forty new dwellings grafted onto its gable ends, in order to take advantage of the empty land around the buildings.

Each existing apartment profits from an increase in surface area of thirty-three square meters and the addition of a winter garden and a balcony, without any major structural works or the organization of the building being affected. Each bathroom was relocated to an existing nine-square-meter bedroom with a window, while a new bedroom was created in an extension and the former bathroom became a storage space. A two-meter-wide climate control device, consisting of moveable transparent panels with fabric screening, serves as winter gardens. Combined with a one-meter-wide balcony, it is mounted in front of the original facade. The newly constructed apartments, backing onto the existing high-rise, also have a generous amount of space, with winter gardens and balconies.

The transformation, extension, and densification of the block was much more cost effective than the demolition of the forty existing flats and the reconstruction of eighty new ones, and ultimately provided apartments that are more generous than the new standard size in construction.

The project prefigures the total transformation of the area. Developed in other buildings in the area, the principle of densification would permit the construction of 258 new dwellings, the qualitative transformation of 312 flats, and the creation of new local amenities and services, without eating into the large central park.

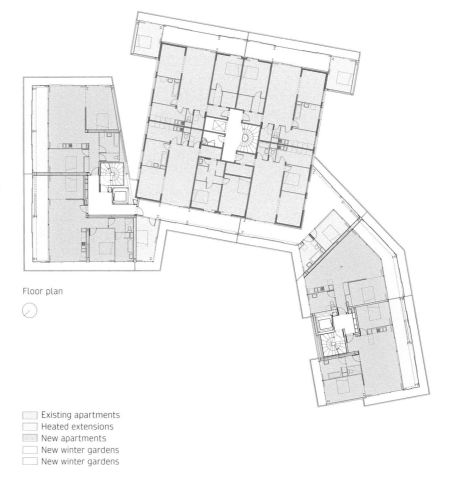

Floor plan

◷

	Existing apartments
	Heated extensions
	New apartments
	New winter gardens
	New winter gardens

The central existing building from the nineteen-seventies was extended with two side wings and winter gardens set in front of the facade. The new apartments will help finance the conversion of the existing building.

The facade of the existing building was broken open to allow access to the new room space, which comprises a winter garden and balcony accessed from each apartment via sliding glass doors.

Right
In the new buildings, both steel constructions, a generous spatial layer was placed in front of the facade as a thermal and acoustic buffer zone, with sliding door elements made of translucent, corrugated polycarbonate that open onto the surrounding balconies.

Plan for the inventory transformation process

1 Removal of asbestos coatings
2 Dismantling of window and wall element
3 Dismantling of balcony
4 Dismantling of window parapet
5 Additional and enlarged room (12.5 m²)
6 Enlarged bathroom (9.45 m²) by reclaiming one room
7 Dismantling of the partition walls possible to enlarge the WC, which is now accessible for the disabled
8 New winter garden as extension of the living space and the balcony
9 Glass railings
10 Polycarbonate elements, translucent and movable, and sun curtains
11 Sliding window, double glazing, 2/3 opening
12 Thermal curtain (winter/summer)
13 Use of the existing exterior walls as structural support for the new annexes by removing asbestos panels

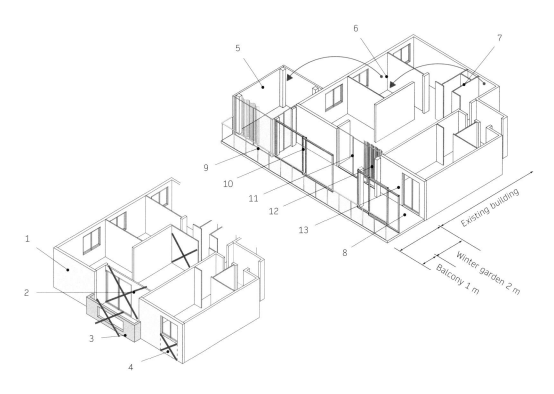

127

Regine Leibinger

Barkow Leibinger, Berlin, Germany
Apartment House Prenzlauer Berg, Berlin, Germany, 2016

This remarkable apartment house was created in the inner courtyard of a Wilhelminian perimeter block development. With a steep, ten-meter high roof, the unconventionally shaped building is covered in a multicolored brick skin, which flows smoothly from the vertical to the sloping surfaces, without joints. At first glance, it does not fit the idea of contextual expansion; yet it, in fact, adheres to building and preservation regulations by integrating the building into its surroundings whilst retaining an independent character.

The preservation authorities, which became involved because of the need to protect the existing ensemble, wanted a new building within the cubature of the transverse building destroyed in the war. However, this was refused by the building supervision authorities due to the current regulations on clearance areas. This was solved by deploying an extremely low-set roof with an eaves height of about only seven-and-a-half meters and an inclination of almost seventy degrees; this extends over three stories to the top of the building at about eighteen meters, where a roof terrace cuts off the top of the pyramid. This cubature allowed the prescribed distances to the three sides of the neighboring properties to be maintained. Like its predecessor, the almost square building is flush with the firewall of the neighboring transverse building.

The exposed exterior masonry of the double shell construction references the Wilhelminian style of construction and the materiality of the front building's street facade. For this purpose, 20,000 bricks in six different colors were produced in a Brandenburg brick factory. The production and storage traces created or left behind before the firing process means the stones are unique. They were set with high precision, especially on the sloping surfaces, and in an arbitrary pattern.

The irregularly proportioned windows with aluminum frames are a reminder of the often industrial use of the block interiors at the time they were created. Their wide frames are flush with the building structure. Metallically shimmering, smooth, and sharp-edged, they create a feature in the brick facade that stands out; they loosen the strict geometry of the building. Two residential units are each laid out as maisonettes one above the other. The lower unit (a good 250 square meters) is divided into a ground floor living area with a garden and the bedrooms on the first floor. The attic apartment (almost 200 square meters) extends over four floors and includes a roof terrace. The communal staircase, the stairs within the units, and the auxiliary and technical facility rooms are compactly aligned along the fire wall.

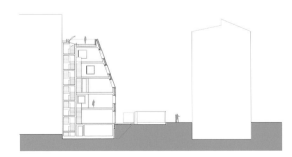
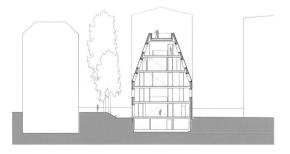

Cross and longitudinal section

The pyramid-shaped residential building, hidden in the inner courtyard of a Wilhelminian-period perimeter block structure in Berlin, came about as a result of the strict building regulations and rules regarding the preservation of historical monuments.

The attic apartment of ca. 200 m²
comprises four levels: two for living,
one for sleeping, and a roof terrace.

The lower unit of ca. 250 m² is divided
into a ground level living floor with
a garden in the courtyard and several
bedrooms on the second floor.

Lu Wenyu (right) and Wang Shu

Lu Wenyu

Amateur Architecture Studio, Hangzhou, China
Ningbo Museum of Art, Ningbo, China, 2005

The project is located on the north bank of the Yong River in the Ningbo Port area. The whole harbor area was reworked after the shipping industry was moved to another site. As part of an overall plan to protect this historic block, the waiting room of the former port was turned into a large modern art museum. The idea was initially to preserve the building, a legacy of the nineteen-eighties; however, as construction progressed, it was discovered that during previous reconstruction work, the building had been seriously damaged and no longer adhered to the modern architectural regulations in China. Thus the architects decided to demolish the whole building, except for a beacon tower. It was also agreed to preserve the interior's special pattern, which was part of the city's shared memory, because the building has once been a place where the people in Ningbo set off by ship for Shanghai or, as pilgrims, for the holy land of Buddhism, Putuoshan.

The final construction plan contains multiple design clues underlining this connection. It first reduplicated the relationship between the port and the ship with a high platform and the building's maritime form. Two loading stages are situated roughly in the same place as the former air-landing stage. It also reduplicated the relationship between the local traditional courtyard and the building. From the street, access to the museum is via the high platform. There is no magnificent square or broad steps—something which has become the most controversial part of the design.

The building, as is traditional in populous China, offers facilities both below and above ground. The lower part is the "economical foundation," including a garage that can hold 150 cars. The hall for temporary exhibitions in the basement of the main hall can host various commercial exhibition activities, which helps to solve the problem that many museums in China have (construction funds but no operating funds). The upper part of the building is exclusively for art exhibitions and accompanying events. The materials used also reveal further pointers to the past. The gray brick in the foundation was the main building material of the former block; the steel and timber in the upper part were the main materials in port and ships. There is a group of caves along the river with figures of Buddha to remind people that the building was once the place where pilgrims set out for the holy island of Putuoshan.

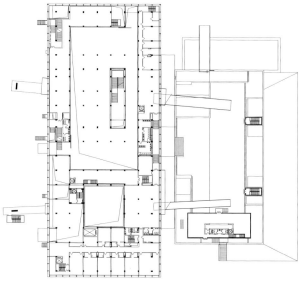

Floor plan, upper floor

The design for a museum on the banks of the Yong River contains numerous references to the harbor building, which had to make way for the new building despite efforts to preserve it. The relationship to the harbor was thematized in the construction of two access walkways located at the site of the former landing stages, among other things.

The motif of landing bridges was also adopted for the connection between the front and rear structures. The lighthouse in the background is the only building of the former complex that has been preserved.

Both buildings are divided into two parts,
which are also financially connected:
the basement, which serves as a garage
and temporary hall for commercial
exhibition activities, co-finances the floor
above for art exhibitions.

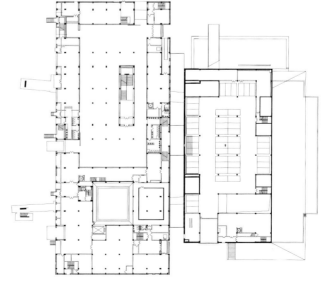

Floor plan, first floor

Dorte Mandrup

Dorte Mandrup, Copenhagen, Denmark
The Wadden Sea Center Ribe, Denmark, 2017

Located in the southern part of Jutland, Denmark, The Wadden Sea is Denmark's largest national park and a UNESCO World Heritage site. Around 12,000 years ago, the end of the Ice Age created a 500-kilometer-long coastal area we now call the Wadden Sea. The area has seen the tide come and go for millions of years, creating unique marshlands. It is virtually impossible not to be inspired by this ancient natural scenery.

Dorte Mandrup has created a one-of-a-kind building that pays homage to the regional material and traditional craftsmanship of the Wadden Sea. The Center, which was inaugurated in February 2017, is an interpretation of the local building tradition and the rural farmhouse typology significant in the area, and perfectly adapted to the surrounding landscape. The building is designed as a gateway for visitors to the Wadden Sea region that sees fifteen million birds stop by its mudflats each year, as they refuel on their journey along the East Atlantic Flyway migration route.

The main concept of the architecture is a new sculptural interpretation of the existing building culture of the region. The extension increases the space within to 2,800 square meters, encompassing over 1,000 square meters of exhibition space, meeting and teaching facilities, a café and shop. The Center is erected with thatched roofs and facades, hereby underlining the tactile qualities and robustness that can be found in the traditional crafts and materials of the region. Straw for the thatching was harvested from the nearby fjords. During its drying process, the thatch takes on salt from the sea air.

Since its opening in 2017, the Wadden Sea Center's higher visitor numbers have shown the increasing interest in migrating birds, oysters, and thatch. Around 91,000 guests visited the Center in 2019. The main goal of the institution is to create awareness and understanding for the marshland and the Wadden Sea. The architecture is sustainable, visionary, and bold, and brings forth the center as a didactic information hub of the future.

1 Entrance
2 Wardrobe
3 Service area
4 Cinema
5 Exhibition

Longitudinal and cross section

For the design of the new building and conversion of the three-winged courtyard, which was built in 1995, Dorte Mandrup took advantage of local building traditions and materials, such as wood and reed.

The Departure, an art installation consisting of 500 LCDs as a metaphor for the flight of birds, on show in one of the exhibition rooms. Subdued light enters the room through a frosted glass window.

1,000 m² of exhibition space are distributed over seven rooms.

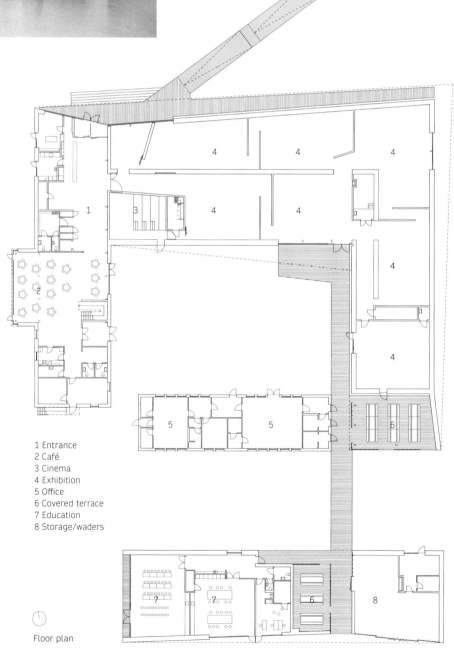

1 Entrance
2 Café
3 Cinema
4 Exhibition
5 Office
6 Covered terrace
7 Education
8 Storage/waders

Floor plan

The existing building was extended, provided with larger openings and clad with narrow robinia wood slats. The shape of its roof was adapted to that of the new building, thus creating a coherent ensemble in which old and new are only subtly distinguishable from one another.

Rozana Montiel

Rozana Montiel Estudio de Arquitectura, Mexico City, Mexico
Common Unity, Mexico City, 2016

Grassroots solutions are necessary in housing projects like this one; change must come from the streets and houses—from the bottom up. Through on-site analyses and experiments, together with the community living here, small projects can make an important contribution. They can become a platform for the exchange of intelligent solutions.

Common Unity is a public space rehabilitation project in the San Pablo Xalpa housing unit in Mexico City. The main objective was to transform a "sectored housing unit" into a "Common Unity," designing with the community and not just for the community, based on the implementation of different actions. The strategy of the project was to work with the "barriers" created by the inhabitants: permeate them, democratize them, and re-signify them to generate unity in the neighborhoods. Through participatory planning, our design strategy substituted dividing vertical structures for sheltering horizontal ones.

By taking a placemaking approach, we transformed the alienated sectors of the housing complex into a community of barrios—which we termed Common Unity. We worked around the physical barriers created by the residents in common areas to make them permeable, democratic, and meaningful. We implemented roof modules equipped for a diverse program with blackboards, climbing walls, handrails, and nets. The new design spoke for itself: residents agreed to remove 90 percent of the barriers and the recovered public space became an extension of each apartment. The new space facilitated a different kind of ownership and appropriation, one that encourages inhabitants to work for the common good.

The strategy proved that it was effective, as people came together to contribute to the redesign of their unit. A change in the perception of the public space was achieved, which came to light when the neighbors themselves requested the removal of fences to take advantage of their outdoor spaces filling them with life. By creating micro-cultural spaces within the housing units, we are facilitating the emergence of a local culture that forms a community.

Visualization of the playground typology, which is intended to turn the inner courtyards of existing complexes into community areas.

1 Four multipurpose ceilings
2 New floors and maintenance
  of green areas
3 "A library" reconstruction
4 Murals between existing walls
5 Playground
6 Lighting
7 Benches and trash cans installation

4   6 7 1   2   6   4   3   6   5   1   2

With the dismantling of the elements separating the courtyard and the construction of an elevated and partially covered platform, a new meeting place is created in the center of the apartment block.

Playground elements are integrated
into the partially roofed steel structure.

Thanks to the planting of tall trees, the site is pleasantly shaded.

Right
The site allows for a variety of appropriations by the residents, such as the use of the platform as a covered open-air cinema.

Kathrin Moore

MooreUrban Design, San Francisco, US
Da Nang Towards 2025 Vision Plan, Da Nang, Vietnam, 2006

As Vietnam's third largest city, Da Nang is anticipating significant development investment together with inevitable growth. To preserve its unique character and cultural values, while remaining competitive as it modernizes and advances the mandate to become a Green City, the Vision Plan explores concepts for Da Nang to become a future-oriented and environmentally sustainable city. Structured like a general plan update, the Da Nang Vision Plan Towards 2025 is comprehensive and strives to create a legacy.

To reduce congestion and pollution, improve city efficiency and maintain public health, Da Nang will need to prepare for major street network improvements together with a full range of alternative transportation options. A multi-modal transportation system will be essential. One proposed mode of mass transportation is Bus Rapid Transit (BRT), which is easily adaptable to the existing network of roads. The system includes also Light Rail Transit (LRT), to connect Da Nang City's growth to the north towards Hue and its regional growth to the south, towards Hoi An.

As investment in Vietnam's central region intensifies, the demand for growth will shift towards the urban center of Da Nang, where a large segment of the rural population will realize economic opportunities for employment, together with opportunities for quality housing, healthcare, and education. The city has a suitable basic structure of streets and block sizes that will easily be adaptable to the principles of "walkable neighborhoods," a concept that needs to be adopted as the basic building block to make the future city attractive to its inhabitants. Da Nang City needs to find a balance between densification and those amenities that will shape quality of life in 2025.

Located between the sea and the mountains, Da Nang has beautiful beachfronts, mountains as a backdrop to the west, and its downtown spans both sides of the Han River. Da Nang's downtown, together with its large urban parks and informal open spaces, creates a green setting. In the future, Da Nang's urban green spaces will need to serve a dual function. The citywide, connected system of open spaces will range from small neighborhood gardens to large parks and major event open spaces. These open spaces will also have to incorporate flood control measures, together with natural filtration and water recycling systems that help mitigate air and water pollution and reduce urban run-off.

On the east bank of the Han River, a less densely developed neighborhood extends like a narrow peninsula between the sea and the river.

The land-use plan shows the various uses envisaged under the Master Plan 2025.

- Mixed-use high-density, commercial
- Mixed-use medium-density, residential
- Medium to low-density, residential
- Low-density residential
- Existing mixed-use
- Resort
- Institutional
- University
- Industry
- Office park
- Port
- Airport
- Airport support
- Open space: park & greenway
- Open space: golf course
- Open space: ecological preserve & agriculture

The west bank of the city along the Han River with new
office towers in front of the historic city district, which is to
be preserved.

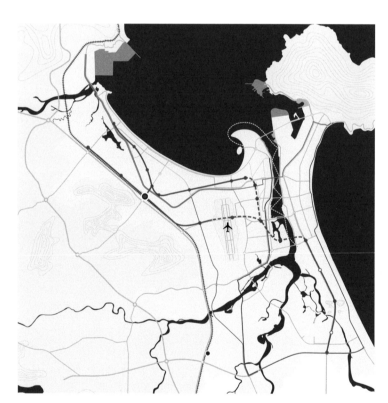

The plan shows the interaction of the
different means of transport as a multi-
modal transportation system.

The circles represent neighborhoods
in which the local center can always
be reached within a maximum of eight
minutes on foot. This concept of "walkable neighborhoods" is the basic building
block of Da Nang's sustainable, future-oriented development.

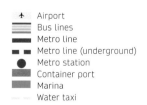

✈ Airport
　　Bus lines
　　Metro line
▪ ▪ Metro line (underground)
● Metro station
　　Container port
　　Marina
　　Water taxi

The master plan includes the preservation
of the historic city district from the
French colonial era.

Proposed open space framework

Open space: park and greenway
Open space: golf course
Open space: ecological preserve
and agriculture
•••• Green boulevard

Farshid Moussavi

Farshid Moussavi Architecture, London, UK
La Folie Divine, Montpellier, France, 2017

La Folie Divine is the first of two apartment buildings, described as *folies,* which have been commissioned by the City of Montpellier in the eighteenth-century tradition of grand mansions surrounded by gardens. With its compact footprint, the nine-story tower frees the surrounding land and creates a scenic backdrop.

The tranquil site is located in Les Jardins de la Lironde, an urban development on the periphery of Montpellier master planned by Christian de Portzamparc. The City asked how the playful character of a *folie* could be a critical tool for generating a new type of residential architecture. As a typology the *folie* plays with an idea that goes beyond mere practicality. La Folie Divine, through its unique assembly of floor plates, balconies, and structure, provides residents with thirty-six apartment types. Its architecture redefines luxury in three ways: by providing a variety of spatial choices to complement lifestyles; by giving the flexibility to modify the interior as and when required, and thirdly, by offering the freedom to enjoy both interior and exterior spaces in utmost privacy.

The building was designed as a nine-story structure in order to minimize the footprint and provide sea and city views. The rest of the site is used as a garden and for corner apartments which benefit from two aspects and natural cross-ventilation. To minimize the need for building maintenance the envelope is clad in corrugated anodized aluminum metal paneling and glass, while hardwood flooring is used for the balconies.

To provide residents with the option of sub-dividing their apartments, the structure of the building is located along the vertical core, which frees up interior space. Each apartment has consequently acquired a unique layout.

To enable both indoor and outdoor living, all apartments are designed with curvilinear balconies that taper at each end and obviate the need for balcony dividing walls between neighbors. The curvilinear balconies are strategically located so that each one enjoys 180-degree views but never looks into the neighboring balcony. There are four different floor configurations, each with differing balcony locations stacked in alternating order to ensure that neighboring balconies are two levels apart from each other. This minimizes downward views from one neighbor to another and creates the choice of two balcony types throughout the building: a single height balcony, shaded by the level above and designed with exterior curtains for additional privacy and wind protection, and a double-height balcony which benefits from maximum sun exposure and provides the possibility of maintaining taller house plants.

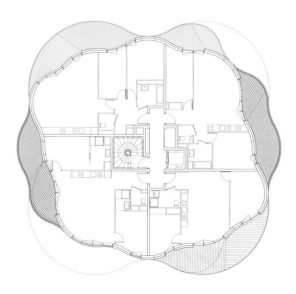

Floor plan, sixth floor. Thanks to a centrally located core, the partition walls within the apartments can be individually determined by the residents.

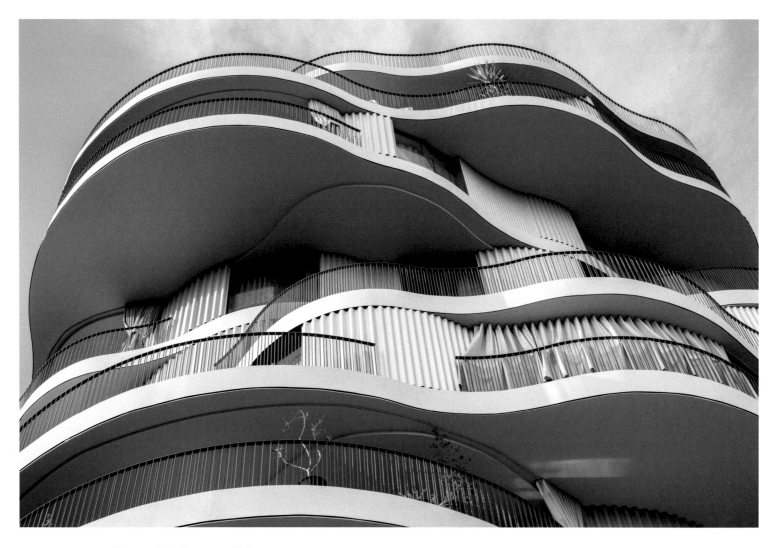

The meandering floors are vertically offset from each other, ensuring maximum privacy on the balconies.

The offset creates roofed, loggia-like
balconies as intimate outdoor spaces.

The tower-like residential building
is one of the highest in the surrounding
area and offers a sweeping view of the
landscape and the sea.

Carme Pinós

Estudio Carme Pinós, Barcelona, Spain
Escola Massana—Art and Design Center, Barcelona, Spain, 2017

The Massana School forms part of the long transformation process of the Gardunya Square, situated in the heart of Barcelona's historical district. Together with the school, the square itself had to be redesigned. Located as it is behind the famous Boqueria Market, it is constantly flooded with tourists. The project needed to meet the requirements of creating a luminous interior made up of open spaces in its 11,000 square meters of usable surface area, while at the same time achieving an exterior that remains in harmony with the urban web in which it stands.

Carme Pinós's architectural design turns the school inward around a skylit interior street or atrium. In a simple scheme, two L-shaped volumes interlock around the atrium. The compositional technique involves rhythmic openings, overlapping angles, large cantilevers, and fragmented massing, which lighten the impact of the building on the neighborhood. The atrium receives direct sunlight throughout the day from different sides. The long sides of the atrium are solid, to reinforce its character as an interior street, with punctured openings for the classroom windows and along the corridors of the workshop wing, while the ground floor is completely open. The skybridges add a Piranesian complexity to the straightforward circulation, enriching the experience of the students' constant movement through the building.

The building is split, both in terms of volumetrics and in the solution used for the facade in response to the surrounding fabric. With the objective of giving it a more unique and sculptural character and simultaneously diminishing bulkiness, the part of the Center that faces the square is decomposed into two rotating volumes that generate different terraces.

Lining the square and the side street, the Art and Design Center's facade consists of a ventilated skin of reddish ceramic louvers, placed in front of the windows, behind which are the art studios and workshops. Reminiscent of a *brise soleil,* the ceramic screening that covers the exterior emphasizes its volumetric aim while at the same time ensuring the student's privacy.

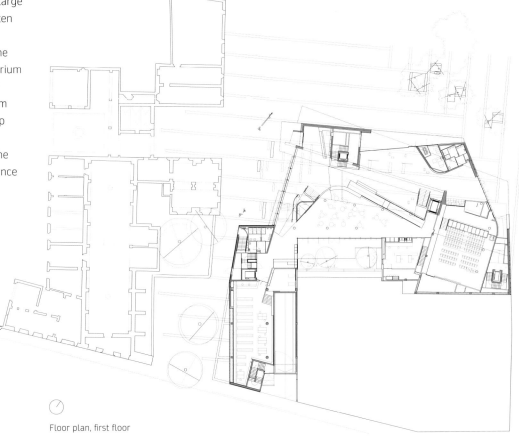

Floor plan, first floor

Two L-shaped sculptural structures interlock around an atrium, which is designed
as an inner, light-flooded street.

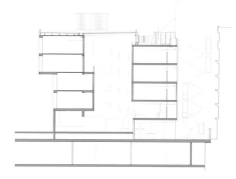

Cross section

Left
Loggias break through the ventilated facade of ceramic lamellas.

Opposite
Free-floating stairs cross the light-flooded atrium that connects the two buildings

Some of the studio rooms, such as the top-floor painting studio shown here, are multistoried. The ceramic lamellas regulate daylight and prevent direct sunlight from entering.

Floor plan, fourth floor

Nili Portugali

Nili Portugali, Tel-Aviv, Israel
Residential building, Tel-Aviv, Israel, 2018

The purpose of architecture, as I see it, is first and foremost to create a human environment for human beings. Yet, modern society has lost the human value and thus created a feeling of alienation between man and his environment. The residential project I designed in Tel-Aviv was built on a site assigned for an ordinary apartment building. Here a fundamentally different approach was generated from my holistic-phenomenological approach to architecture. The intention was, firstly, to create a place where the tenants will feel at home, from the moment they enter the site until they reach their private apartment and, secondly, to create a building that will contribute significantly to the public space in which it is located.

As in any organic system, each building has its own uniqueness and power, but at the same time it always functions as part of a larger environment, and it has a responsibility to its existence and wholeness. At the foundation of all those places in which one feels at home are absolute "physical patterns" that have always been responsible for the dialogue between humans and the environment—to the "feeling" of the place.

The secret concealed within the beauty of a place at any level of scale lies in the details, such as the balconies, the high windows, or the building materials. At the same time, the details are not conceived as a random collection of designed elements, but as a structural part of the whole, deriving from a generative language, in which the building and the interior are one continuous system. The walk from the public street to the private apartment is through a continuous system of open spaces that opens one into another leading gradually to the private apartment, not via an alienated lobby, but through an "internal outdoor street" overlooked by the apartment's facade. The "internal street," to which each of the apartments has direct and private access, was an appropriate solution for isolating the apartments from the busy streets alongside the site. The garden apartments can be reached via a private courtyard and the upper apartments via a private entrance balcony connected to the open stairs and the external elevators, thus creating a sense of connectedness to the ground.

The developer realized that by adopting and trusting this uncommon approach to architecture, he was not only providing a human response to those living in the building and a value to the environment as a whole, but creating a solution that was economically viable—and that despite the building's location at a crossroads of two busy streets.

Nili Portugali

Visualization showing the view from the
street onto the two-part residential complex
with an elongated inner courtyard

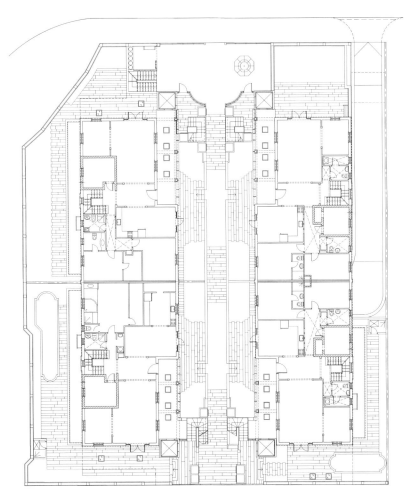

Floor plan, first and second floor

Internal street with the garden flats
and the open stairs leading to the upper
apartments.

Opposite
The stairs lead to arcades from
which the apartments are accessed.

Paula Santos

Paula Santos Arquitectura, Porto, Portugal
Family House, Ovar, Portugal, 2011

This concrete house in Portugal features an indoor swimming pool and a painter's studio. Most rooms in the house are at ground floor level on either side of a long corridor and only an ensuite bedroom is located upstairs. The roof pitches upwards in three places to accommodate this first floor and to give high ceilings to the studio and pool room.

The house at Ovar was a project where we stretched to the limit several ideas and concepts that we had been considering for some time, but which we had never implemented. Given the clients' enthusiasm, it is also—and above all—a project, which enabled us to talk with other people about their own way of inhabiting a dwelling. The large-scale project, covering 640 square meters, located on not very stable sandy soil and in rather uninteresting surroundings, allowed us to ponder the house as an object which develops in a continuum. The need to arrange the main functions of the house on a ground floor meant that the difference between spaces was implemented by means of variable heights in geometric forms. In respect of their importance and meaning, the most expressive areas, such as the swimming pool and the painter's studio or the body of the entrance from the street, acquire more expressive and more elevated forms.

Paved terraces and a grass lawn surround the house, and a concrete canopy provides an outdoor shelter with circular skylights. The idea for the object in concrete, a traditionally sculptable material, appears implicit in this concept, providing the malleable form of the elevations with level and sloping surfaces up to the coverage. The length of the corridor is used to distribute the desired functions and large areas, creating a relation with the terrain, with the other areas, suggesting outdoor leisure, and more or less intimate areas.

The construction is refined and demanding. Detailed planning was of major importance in successfully defining the stereotomy of the elevations designed to be continuous—the ceilings and flooring, the coverages, and the placing of natural light.

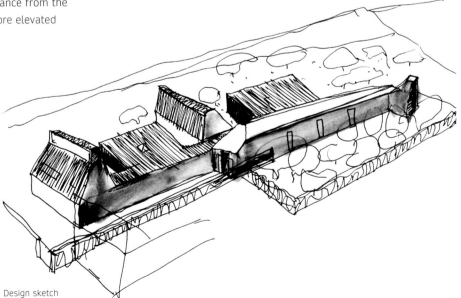

Design sketch

Variously shaped rectangular structures
intertwine with the surrounding exterior
space to form a spatial continuum.

Right
Entrance from the street side with the
expressively designed canopy of exposed
concrete.

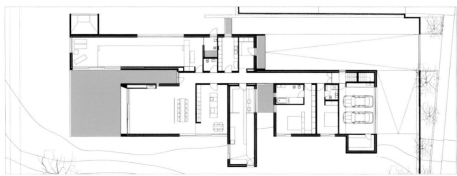

Floor plan, first floor

Large openings break through the sculptural structure, which is made entirely of exposed concrete.

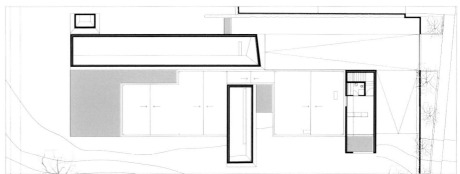

Floor plan, second floor

Kazuyo Sejima

Kazuyo Sejima + Ryūe Nishizawa/SANAA, Tokyo, Japan
Rolex Learning Center, Lausanne, Switzerland, 2009

This is a learning center located at the École poly-technique fédérale de Lausanne (EPFL) campus which includes diverse services such as a library, multi-purpose hall, auditorium, café, restaurant, quiet zones, working places for students and scientists, and offices.

We designed the building as a single space and put it almost in the center of the site for easy access from the surrounding facilities. The rectangular building is loosened up by the undulating parallel course of floor and roof, and appears light and bouncy. The structure, supported by barely visible columns, rises to form two flat hills, which overlook the campus and offer spectacular views of Lake Geneva and the Alps. All services are installed in this big room, a 166.5 meters by 121.5 meters area, which undulates gently, making it a kind of topographical environment. It offers the flexibility to use the building in many ways, now and in the future. These waves create a large amount of openness under the building, inviting people to walk under and approach the entrance hall located at the center of the building.

A total of 190 thin pillars support the roof which runs parallel to the corrugated floor. Glass with a total area of 4,800 square meters between the floor and roof slab forms the outer finish. The curved glass facades have to take the movement of the concrete, each piece of glass is unique and cut separately, and each piece moves independently on jointed frames. The main structural materials are steel and wood with concrete poured into formwork so precisely that the underside of the building looks polished.

The elegant concrete shells span up to fifty meters with a thickness of only thirty to sixty centimeters. The structure is punctuated by fourteen organically shaped openings of varying sizes, five of which are designed as patios, offering outdoor seating. The remaining ones are glazed and provide natural light-ing to the interior spaces and for the visual connec-tion between exterior and interior spaces. Some of the interior work spaces are also screened off by round transparent glass walls.

This landscape with valleys, slopes, and undulations, as well as different-sized light gardens, generates spaces with diverse characteristics. Clusters of small light wells generate a quiet atmosphere for offices, adapted to the human scale. Each space is softly divided but remains continuous at the same time, connected to the campus outside. Our endeavor with these strategies was to create an open structure for people—an intimate and yet public space.

The multifunctional library building is located outside the city in the immediate vicinity of Lake Geneva. The flat, rectangular building forms an undulating landscape, which is broken up by fourteen organically shaped openings of varying sizes.

Site plan

The external wave form of the building also shapes the hills, valleys and plateaus of the open interior, which flows smoothly from one zone to the next, without separating elements.

1 Main entrance
2 Café
3 Food court
4 Bank
5 Bookshop
6 Offices
7 Multipurpose hall
8 Library
9 Work area
10 Ancient books collection
11 Research collection
12 Restaurant

Floor plan

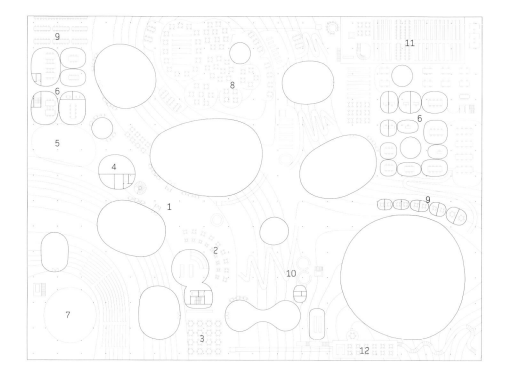

One of five openings, which are designed as walk-in patios and offer opportunities for people to sit outside. The floor of the building consists of polished concrete, which had to be laboriously produced on site. The roof was designed as a light-weight construction in wood and steel.

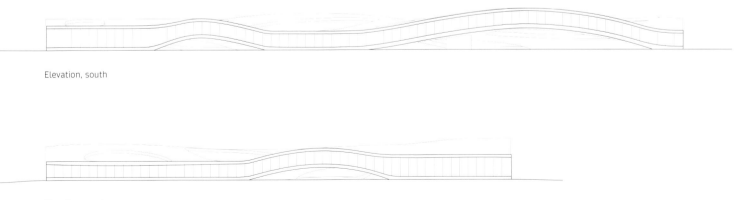

Elevation, south

Elevation, west

Annabelle Selldorf

Selldorf Architects, New York, US
David Zwirner 20th Street, New York, US, 2013

This contemporary art gallery is located in West Chelsea, just one block away from the gallery's other West 19th Street location. The neighborhood's industrial heritage inspired the design's simple monumentality. Made from exposed concrete, the facade has a simultaneously rough and refined expression with a grittiness that resonates with nearby industrial structures and an elegance that creates a distinguished identity for the gallery. The teak storefront and windows provide a warm contrast to the concrete.

The gallery, which covers an area of 2,787 square meters, is built to museum standards and specifically designed to accommodate works by estate artists—including modern masters such as Dan Flavin and Donald Judd as well as earlier masters such as Paul Klee. Gallery spaces are diverse in their scale, materiality, and lighting, offering a flexible range of environments for the wide range of different contemporary art forms. The main exhibition space is an expansive 465-square-meter, column-free gallery. Concrete floors bring an industrial sensibility to the space, along with four north-facing sawtooth skylights. The public exhibition space continues on the second floor with a more intimate series of galleries. The upper levels contain private functions such as viewing rooms, offices, a library, and art handling areas.

Exposed concrete forms the entry spaces as well as the central stair. The board-formed texture appears on atrium walls, while the more delicate stair runs have a smooth finish. Open to each of the five floors, the central staircase creates a counterpoint to the restrained exhibition spaces. The building is permeated with natural light coming via the stair skylight or windows which provide side light for offices, galleries, and showrooms. The building sets a new environmental standard for art-related facilities as the first commercial gallery in the US to receive LEED (Leadership in Energy and Environmental Design) certification. The LEED Gold project incorporates five green roof spaces, mechanical efficiency, maximized daylighting, and locally and responsibly sourced materials.

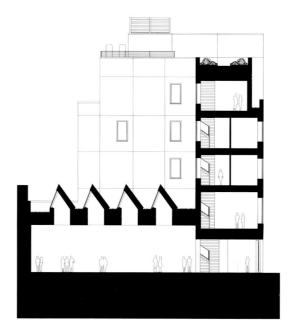

Cross section. The large exhibition room with shed roof and the five-story gallery building facing the street

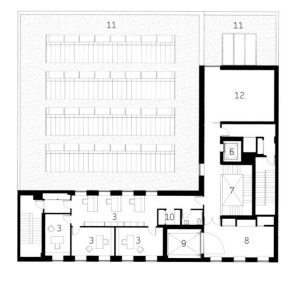

Floor plan, first floor and upper floor

1 Entrance
2 Reception
3 Office
4 Mechanical
5 Gallery
6 Passenger elevator
7 Main staircase
8 Art handling
9 Freight elevator
10 Pantry
11 Green roof
12 Viewing Room

170

Access to the gallery is via a large glazed entrance on the first floor, partly framed with reddish teak.

Left
The purist main staircase provides access to additional, smaller exhibition areas as well as event rooms, offices, a library, and the so-called Viewing Room on the upper floors.

Opposite, top
The large exhibition room on the first floor with a work of art by Donald Judd

Pavitra Sriprakash

Shilpa Architects, Chennai, India
Mahindra World City Club, Chengalpattu, India, 2015

This private club within the Mahindra World City draws from the rich cultural heritage of Kanchipuram and the region, and is designed to create a tranquil retreat. The architectural program leverages its location and proximity to the lake and wraps into its location. The structure comprises lofted spaces to house and host world-class indoor sports.

A freeform was adopted as a response to the geography and to reflect the playfulness and relaxation that the environment provides. The reception area is the first double height space a visitor encounters and its walls are clad with exposed Kandi bricks. This handmade and sundried construction material is typical of the region. It celebrates local architecture and its earthy color, tone, and texture lends a rustic appearance. It contrasts the exposed concrete finishes on the walls and floors of the rest of the club. A green roof and natural lighting provides opportunities to add towards the sustainability factor of the building. The day lighting in most spaces within the club have been maximized based on optimal orientation and site placement of the built form vis-a-vis the open landscape areas. A system of tiered roofs seamlessly envelops the entire club. Landscaped terraces and green roofs allow first-floor occupants to experience greenery apart from the pool-side lawns. Rain chains along the exterior corridors convey rainwater runoff.

Tanjore Art has always been a rich, respected tradition, framed behind glass to enclose and preserve the 24-carat gold and precious stones that adorn the painting. We devised a way for the painting to be coated with a specialized resin to expose the art. The art on the wall complements the curved staircase that resembles the feathers of the majestic peacock. The design weaves in and out in the form of a fan, symbolized by a dancing peacock, to achieve a carefully constructed connection to the natural environment.

Swales are yet another feature that sit as part of the main lawns and offers an efficient ground water recharge system during the monsoon months as well as a solution to prevent flooding. The "fish scale" aqua bands that are part of the facade are an architectural method of conveying rainwater while providing a unique aesthetic.

The bamboo wall, being a rapidly renewable material, is an example of the project's commitment towards sustainability goals. The wind directions were studied in order to give the bamboo a wind chime effect that adds to the musical nature of this material. These dynamic musical walls are planned in areas which have outdoor seating as well, such as the al-fresco reading lounge.

Outdoor area with pool. The blue vertical fish-scale aqua bands on the facade of the building on the right channel rainwater from the roof and facade into water collection troughs in the lawns.

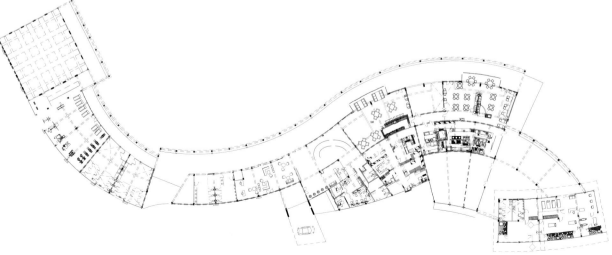

Floor plan, first floor

A pergola provides club guests with a shaded walkway.

The back wall of the two-story lobby is clad with handmade "Kandi bricks" and adorned with a Tanjore artwork typical of southern India.

The stepped roofs of the curved complex were designed to cater to the different spatial requirements of various indoor sports.

Siv Helene Stangeland

Helen & Hard, Stavanger, Norway
Spa for Marina Abramović, outside New York, US, since 2018

The spa in the garden of Marina Abramović's summerhouse outside New York is a small separate house in the shape of a crystal. Her property is dominated by undulating, tree-covered hills and has a river meandering through it, which has created a valley-like formation. Marina wishes to use the spa alone but also bring friends and students from her institute to take part in cleansing and presencing rituals, which she also explores in her artistic work. The spa house comprises of a sauna, steam room, massage room, wardrobes, showers, and a lounge area. Her only more specific wish was that we integrate some of her many large natural crystals, which she collects.

Three different contextual natures have inspired the design language. The sharp, crystalline outer shape of the spa house relates to the existing star-shaped summer house and reveals the theme of crystals in the interior. The inner space shaped like an upside-down basket made of timber relates to the trees in the garden, and a floor of concrete, stone, and rammed earth relates to the geological layers of the ground made visible by the river. The building with circa sixty square meters has all the spa functions organized in niches between the basket and the outer crystalline building envelope. They all face the spectacular central space lounge area with a huge window facing the garden. The timber structure has a very complex geometry, made to hold the many crystals, and will be prefabricated using advanced robotic machinery.

For the organizing principle, a reference is made to the Turkish Hammams, with the hot stone in the middle and the niches around it for different cleansing rituals.

The spa lies like a crystal in the garden
of Marina Abramović. The artist plans
to use it for cleansing and presentation
rituals (visualization).

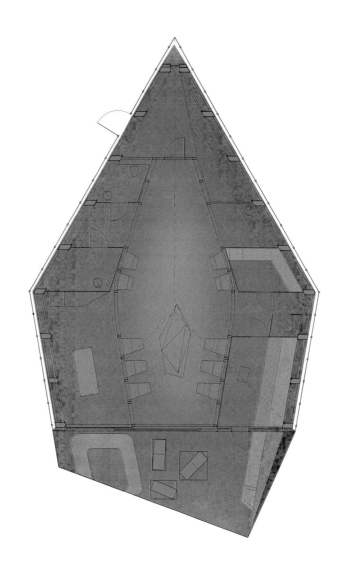

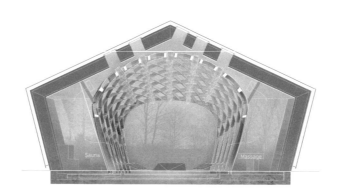

Floor plan and section

Natural crystals collected by the artist
are inserted into the wooden structure of
the bathhouse, where they conduct light
into the central room (visualization).

Brigitte Sunder-Plassmann

Sunder-Plassmann Architekten, Kappeln, Germany
The Museum of Innocence, Istanbul, Turkey, 2011

The Turkish writer and winner of the Nobel Prize for literature Orhan Pamuk bought the tall, narrow town house, built in 1894, in the European district of Beyoğlu, Istanbul thirteen years ago. In the nineteen-seventies he had the idea for a novel to be set in this old Istanbul house. The story is about an unhappy lover who becomes a manic collector of objects, all of which have some connection to his beloved. The objects: postcards, photos, shoes, jewelry, ashtrays, and salt shakers are described in great detail in the novel. These descriptions are typical of the atmosphere that now prevails in the museum. By providing a look at life inside the walls of upper-class Istanbul in the late twentieth century, the museum presents a piece of Istanbul's cultural history.

Sunder-Plassmann Architekten built the Museum of Innocence in this old town house, in cooperation with product designer Carlotta Werner and artist Johanna Sunder-Plassmann. They developed the building and exhibition concept according to the novel in close collaboration with its author Orhan Pamuk. After the detailed design phase, the team took over the building, which had already been gutted and fitted with an earthquake-proof steel structure. The story takes place in the European district of Beyoğlu, which is, so to speak, the foyer of the museum and thus part of the exhibition. The museum building itself is a small, listed residential building from 1894, four and a half meters wide and fifteen meters long. Three floor slabs were inserted, connected to each other by an atrium in the middle.

Based on the collection of objects described in the novel and the eighty-three chapters of the book, the exhibition was arranged in eighty-three showcases and develops chronologically along the walls up to the third floor.

The project was conceived as a balance between modern museum architecture and dark, traditional wooden furniture, with the exhibits interacting with daylight and artificial light. The building itself recedes more and more as the objects illuminated in the showcases dominate the space and retell the fictional story of the novel in a three-dimensional way. The Museum of Innocence, which won the Museum of the Year Award in 2014, is a work in progress. Orhan Pamuk will no doubt continue expanding the unfinished collection with new objects from the novel.

In collaboration with writer Orhan Pamuk, the narrow, listed, old town house in Beyoğlu, the European quarter of Istanbul, was converted and expanded into a museum.

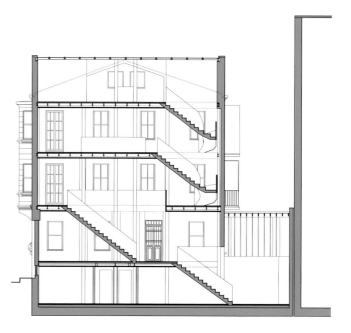

Longitudinal section

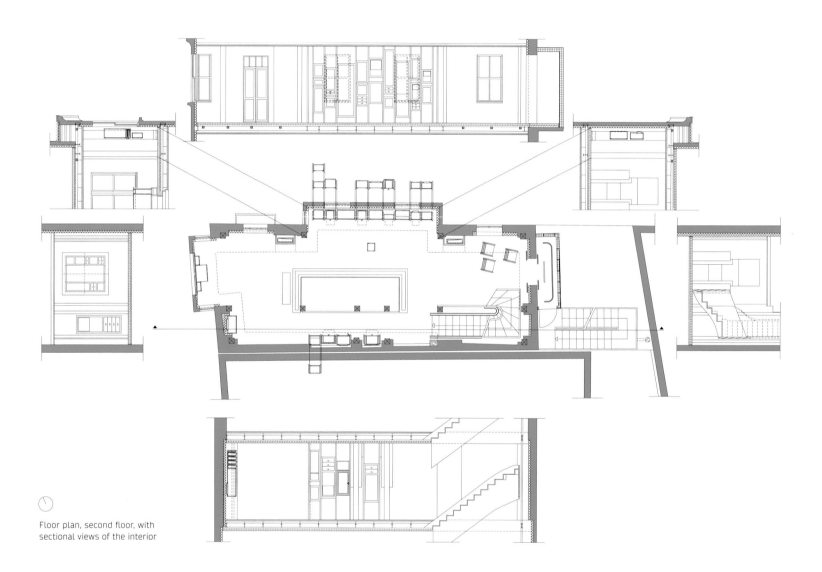

Floor plan, second floor, with
sectional views of the interior

The exhibits on the upper floor are presented in ceiling-height display cases that make optimal use of the available space.

View from the second floor through the narrow atrium staircase to the first floor

Lene Tranberg

Lundgaard & Tranberg Arkitekter, Copenhagen, Denmark
The Tietgen Dormitory, Copenhagen, Denmark, 2005

The Tietgen Dormitory is an interesting example of a visionary client and a visionary program for a dormitory for 360 young people. However, the context was challenging because of an uncompleted rigid urban structure under construction at the same time—part of the development of the Ørestad area close to Copenhagen city center. The only given quality was the nature with its open flat grassland.

The challenge for this project was to make a place that could serve as a "social condenser," balancing and respecting both the individual and the community. At the same time, we wanted to be able to enrich the urban life in the new development, by the intense presence of young people and thus help to create an active community.

Intuitively we started looking at circular structures. By using a circular geometry, we could work with an additive system of equal units all facing the surroundings. The system almost seems organic and airy with a huge relief catching the shifting light.

All communal functions face the courtyard—a communal kitchen, a study room, and a depot. All the units consist of the same module with twelve people in every group, divided by a staircase, an elevator, and a terrace. They are connected by an internal continuing daylight-infused corridor with a view of the courtyard. A plywood wall runs along the entire corridor with an integrated textile artwork in different grade of nuances to give the space a warm glow and a subtle identity—integrating doors and numbers, running along into all units. There the wall becomes a living and a storage wall, integrating a small bathroom and serving as a room divider. A wardrobe on wheels makes it possible for students to shape their own space for sleeping and studying. A place to rest, to focus, and retreat.

The entire ground floor is elevated on huge concrete frames to make a flexible space for all communal functions, opening up towards the surroundings and the courtyard. To make the light touch the building and the interiors in a deeper tone, we developed a rhythmical play with the same system of extending walls in the common units—like notes on a line of notes. We chose natural, robust materials treated with care to reveal their natural character with a smooth and soft surface. The skin of the entire building is an alloy of tin and copper, a material with a long life that patinates well and gather the excessive expression of the entire structure into a calm, complete entity.

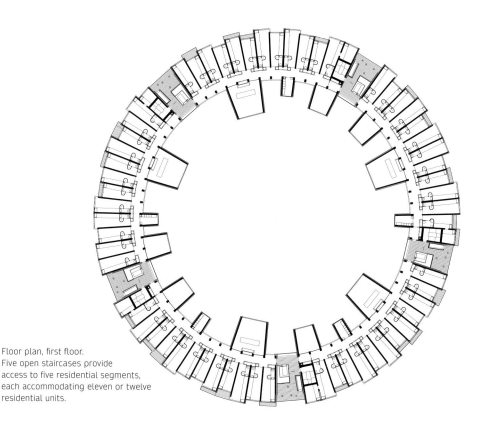

Floor plan, first floor.
Five open staircases provide access to five residential segments, each accommodating eleven or twelve residential units.

An "inverse" spatial organization thwarts the possible problems of a ring-shaped residential complex: the interior is turned inside out, with the private rooms facing the outer facade. The first-floor zone is reserved for the administration and for common areas such as workshops and fitness rooms.

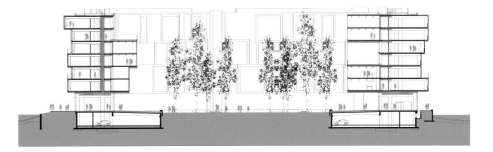

Section

Interplay of viewing between the open
staircases and the roof terraces
of the cantilevered common rooms

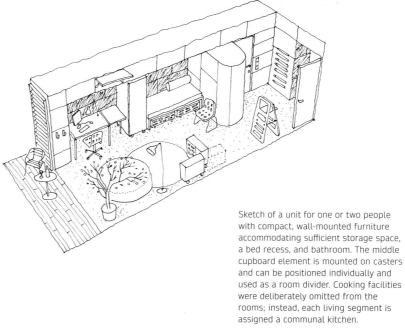

Sketch of a unit for one or two people
with compact, wall-mounted furniture
accommodating sufficient storage space,
a bed recess, and bathroom. The middle
cupboard element is mounted on casters
and can be positioned individually and
used as a room divider. Cooking facilities
were deliberately omitted from the
rooms; instead, each living segment is
assigned a communal kitchen.

The social life of the dormitory takes place
inside the circle—in the cantilevered
community cubes, on the terraces, and
in the inner courtyard.

Billie Tsien

Tod Williams Billie Tsien Architects and Partners, New York, US
The American Folk Art Museum, New York, US, 2001 (demolished in 2014)

The American Folk Art Museum was an idiosyncratic home for idiosyncratic art. A twelve-meter-wide by thirty-meter-long site on 53rd Street was the institution's home. Completed in 2001, the eight-story building was the first new museum to be built in New York City in more than three decades.

Four upper floors were devoted to gallery space for permanent and temporary exhibitions. A small café overlooked 53rd Street from the mezzanine. To accommodate the program, the building extended two levels below ground. The first held the auditorium and classrooms, the second housed the museum's offices, library, and archive. At street level was the museum store, accessible during non-museum hours via a separate entrance.

A skylight above a grand staircase between the second and third floors filled adjacent galleries with natural light. Openings at each level allowed daylight to filter down to the lowest floor, animating interior spaces with ever-changing light. Much of the flooring was terrazzo ground concrete, linking to the walls which were concrete as well. The flooring for the gallery juxtaposed the cold feeling of concrete with Ruby Lake fir logs. Art was built into the structure and its circulation paths. In addition to the gallery spaces, a series of niches presented a more permanent selection of art objects. Visitors could choose from different routes to move through the building.

The museum was surrounded on three sides by the Museum of Modern Art (MoMA). Its facade made a quiet statement of independence. Metal panels of white bronze, cast at an art foundry, covered the building's exterior. Variation within the panels' surface was achieved by casting them from sand molds taken from the texture of concrete. When liquid tombasil, an unorthodox copper-bronze is poured onto a mold of either concrete or stainless steel, chemical reactions between the two different surfaces and the molten metal lead to irregularities in color and texture. Each of the sixty-three panels comprising the facade was therefore unique. Sculptural in form, the facade recalled an abstracted open hand. Its panels folded inward to create a faceted plane.

In 2011 MoMA had already bought the property from the Folk Art Museum, which was suffering from a lack of funds. The MoMA decided to demolish the museum, despite protests, as the design did not match that of MoMA. An architectural gem for New York City was demolished in 2014 and covered by an extension of the MoMA, designed by Diller, Scofidio & Renfro. Prior to demolition, the panels that had made up the facade of the American Folk Art Museum were removed and stored by the MoMA.

The facade was made of white bronze plates containing copper, which were cast as unique pieces in sand molds. They shone in different colors and intensities depending on the incidence of light and orientation.

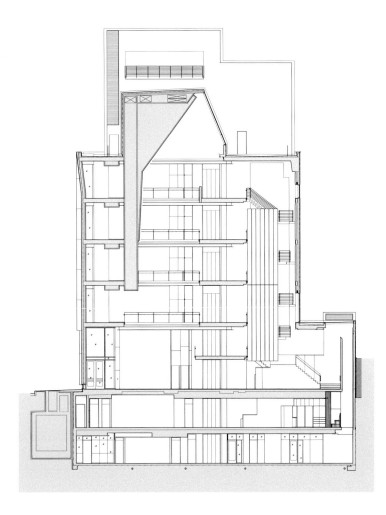

Longitudinal section. Due to restrictions on the maximum permissible above-ground construction volume and construction height for an extensive program, various functions, such as an auditorium, work rooms, offices, a library, and archives, had to be accommodated in two basement levels.

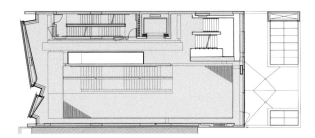

Floor plan, second floor

With the light distributed from the very top to the very bottom of the building, the atrium created a visual connection between the various floors.

Right
Art was exhibited in access areas throughout the building.

Elisa Valero

elisavalero, Granada, Spain
8 Experimental Apartments, Granada, Spain, 2011

This experimental work is the fruit of research into new low-cost, low-energy construction systems made out of concrete. Concrete is the most widely used composite material and second most used material in the world, after water. The use of a local, easily available material with very good structural behavior could provide high quality, low-cost housing to large sectors of the population.

The experimental housing is situated at the end of a small street that culminates in stairs, like many others on the western slope of the Alhambra. The whole complex is located in a neighborhood of Jewish origin called the Realejo, one of the oldest in the city of Granada. Eight apartments, all different, tailored to the needs of each owner, were built for a neighbors' cooperative around a garden, whose wisteria and virgin vine unite with the adjoining gardens, climbing the brick wall that separates them. The pavement is perforated with small holes in a regular pattern, so that the rainwater can escape back into the ground. At some points the holes change in size to allow for the planting of small trees or plants.

For the construction, the innovative Elesdopa system with its double walls was used. The vertical and horizontal walls provide both structure and enclosure, with thermal insulation in the interior, eliminating any need for additional finishing work. This means a substantial reduction in the amount of concrete used and in the building costs of the work as well as an improvement in the seismic behavior. The walls, floors, and ceilings are all in structural concrete. By designing in accordance with bioclimatic principles, energy costs are reduced and the building itself is almost zero energy because of the continuous insulation, high thermal inertia, and adequate orientations. Structural pillars can be eliminated so full continuity between the garden and the parking area under the building is given.

Structural optimization, coherence, and internal order are good allies in architecture. We do not renounce the most valuable material, light. The lighter and the heavier must be combined to achieve excellence. We seek to create a form of architecture that is as simple as possible, one solving the complexity of real problems; the main commitment of architecture today is not to replace the beauty of Nature, but to save it.

This experimental building is not perfect and we had to learn how to solve new problems during the building process. We still have a long way to go, but we are working towards a more environmentally committed architecture, an architecture within everyone's reach, an architecture that will lead us to a fairer society. Architecture is a risky game. What would be the reward in life if we didn't take the risk and explore new paths?

The interiors are exposed concrete, and the large windows are designed as viewing boxes that slide into the interior.

Floor plan, third floor

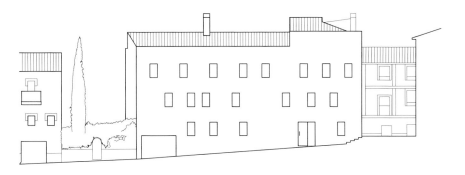

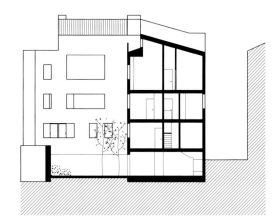

Elevation, street and cross section of the street-side wing with view of the transverse building from the garden side

The building's exterior is restrained, with smaller openings and a minimal facade design that hardly reveals anything of the interior's spatial complexity.

Bottom
The building is located in the Realejo district on the western slope of the Alhambra, and its white facade blends in with its surroundings.

Opposite
No supports were needed for this sculptural space thanks to the concrete construction of the walls, ceilings, and floors.

Nathalie de Vries

MVRDV, Rotterdam, Netherlands
Book Mountain, Spijkenisse, Netherlands, 2012

For a city library in the small town of Spijkenisse, near Rotterdam, we designed a building that wants to be a beacon for the written word. Our Book Mountain project is just what the name suggests: a mountain of bookcases encased in glass, showing off its role to anybody who sees it. Its visibility and inviting presence are significant in a community and in an era where people read less. The library has an important function to invite, especially children, to experience the joy of reading. Since the library is on top of a commercial plinth, extra effort had to be made to create an attractive entrance, as well as good visibility for it.

Located in the center of Spijkenisse, the 9,300-square-meter library takes pride of place on the market square, facing the historic village church from which it appears as a vast mountain of books. In addition to the library, the building houses an environmental education center, a chess club, an auditorium, meeting rooms, commercial offices, and retail space. The pitched roof, that follows the maximum building envelope, references by accident traditional Dutch farmhouses, a reminder of the town's agricultural heritage erased by forty years of expansion.

To accommodate the additional functions required, commercial space and parking facilities were installed in the podium upon which the pyramid is built. More specialized areas such as the auditorium and seminar rooms comprise the core of the pyramid, with the library areas occupying the terraces around, thus taking full advantage of the light and volume provided by the glass roof. The book platforms are connected by wide balconies which in turn are linked to flights of stairs that form a continuous spiraling route around the mountain. It culminates at its peak where a lounge and a café offer panoramic views over the Spijkenisse.

In order to embed the building within its historical context and distinguish between commercial and public programs a "blanket" of brick is laid over the town square, adjacent buildings, and the library's pyramidal heart, covering floors, ceilings, and doors. Above this, the public realm extends to the top of the mountain. Bookshelves that are out of reach distinguish, and literally divide, the library's archive as well as the written off borrowing collections.

The library's bookshelves are made from recycled plastics. The shelves are sustainable, affordable, and even fireproof. They provide a functional background for the books by forming banisters, parapets, information desk, and bar. They constitute another element in the building's palette of recycled materials: brick, wood, and glass. The intensive use of wood for the construction, as well as the heat-regaining warming and cooling system further characterize the library's sustainable design.

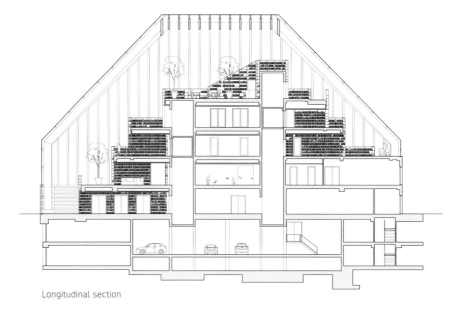

Longitudinal section

The arrangement of the bookshelves mirrors the shape of the building: they are stacked like a pyramid inside, concealing the library's functional rooms. Visitors can climb the "mountain" and, once they reach the top, browse through the books they have picked up in a café.

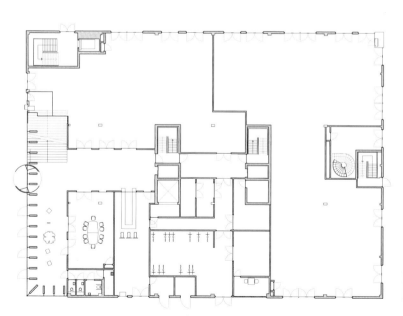

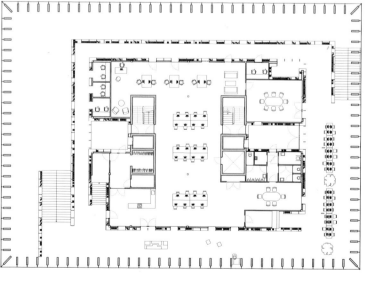

Floor plans, first floor and third floor

The wood mullion-transom facade covered in a glass skin creates a warm atmosphere in the interior.

Right
With its pyramid-shaped roof and transparent glass facade, the building lights up the market square of Spijkenisse in the evening.

Opposite, top
Retreat to a recessed corner among the bookshelves. The shelf walls were made of recycled plastic.

Andrea Wandel

Wandel Lorch Architekten, Saarbrücken, Germany
Evangelisches Landeskirchenamt, Munich, Germany, 2015

The aim of the new Evangelisches Landeskirchenamt (Bavaria's Protestant Church headquarters) was to present an appropriate contemporary solution that neither copies tradition nor negates context, thus fulfilling its cultural and historical responsibility. Located in the vicinity of Maxvorstadt with its valuable, historically charged monuments, such as the buildings of Friedrich von Thiersch and Oswald Biber, the concept also dealt intensively with the dimension of time. The absorption and transformation of various elements is the central idea behind the design.

At a first glance, an apparently traditional, massive structure with a tectonic, perforated facade confidently completes the ensemble of church buildings in the Katharina-von-Bora-Strasse. The historical facades of the surrounding area include massive, partially embossed plinths made of natural stone, elemental plastered facades and saddle or hip roofs that strive for compliance with the logic and design of the district.

At a second glance, the viewer perceives a paradigm shift of the individual building components towards a contemporary, independent building whose entire shell is structured. The story-high mineral base and the flush-fitted baffle plates form a robust base. The upper floors stand out clearly from the base as a felted plaster facade and incorporate the material logic of the context into the new building. The sloping roof surfaces are interrupted and not only allow the attic to be used as a high-quality hall with an open-air space, but also permit the greening of the roof terrace. The shape of the roof gives the entire building the archetypal character of Maxvorstadt.

The paradigm shift and the interaction of the historical and contemporary design of the material lie in the three-dimensional geometric imprint. In addition to its beautiful interplay of light and shadow, the surface, designed in the manner of a fold, is not purely ornamental. It creates a segmented facade, interrupts the stringency of the gridded perforations, allows it to patinate appropriately, and thus forms an important constructive and functional level of the building.

Made of poured, exposed concrete, the base supports the massiveness of the house and takes on the motif of an embossed plinth. On the upper floors, the geometry of the facade is scaled and gives the building more lightness. The lightly plastered, felted surface made of thirty-millimeter, milled silicate panels avoids the monotony of a perforated facade while creating a superior system.

The roof completes the vertical triad of the building structure as a silhouette. With time, the interspersed greenery will complete the outer facades.

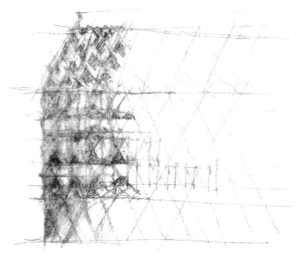

Design sketch of the facade
for the competition

Bavaria's Protestant Church Headquarters, with its existing complex of classicist buildings, gained an extension that echoes the typical features of its neighbors: an embossed plinth, a perforated facade with upright window formats, and a flat hipped roof.

Faceted polygonal elements made
of exposed concrete on the ground floor
and milled silicate polygonal panels on
the upper floors give the facade structure
and depth. The perforated, grid-like
folding structure of the roof continues
and picks up the structure of the facade.

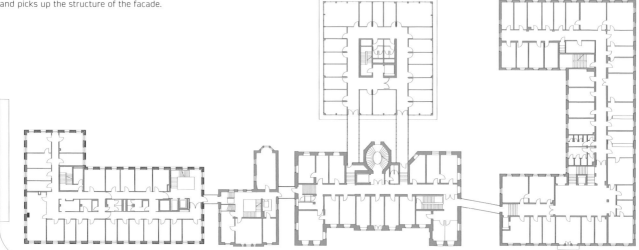

Floor plan with new building (left)
and adjoining existing buildings

202

The large hall and its adjoining terrace are located on the top floor under the open structure of the roof, where the polygonal facets of the facade continue as a grid.

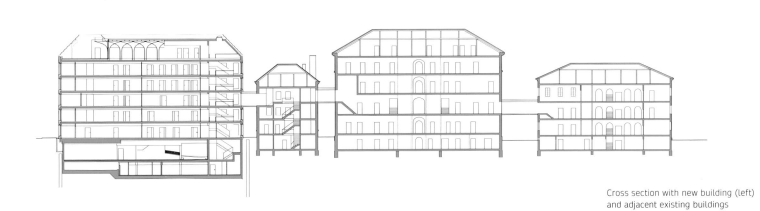

Cross section with new building (left) and adjacent existing buildings

Helena Weber

Berktold Weber Architekten, Dornbirn, Austria
House Built on Rock, Rheintal, Austria, 2015

The house is located above the valley, embedded in natural scenery full of character, and in the vicinity of residential buildings. In this context, the house fits in as a quiet structure, built with local materials and using local resources. The typology of the building was developed to meet today's requirements; an adaptation of the floor plan is planned for the future.

Set on a slope, the building presents a diverse spatial landscape on two levels. With just a few architectural gestures, a space has been created that offers not only protective retreats but also room sequences with generous openings facing towards the valley and wonderful views. A protected entrance leads into the house on the slope side. From here, a spatial continuum opens up, zoned for various uses: a sequence of interwoven interiors and exteriors of varying quality. To the south, the terrace, which offers protection from summer heat, extends in front of the building and enhances the interior with generous glazing. The covered terrace deck adjoins the dining area in the southwest and offers a view of the valley. From here the upper garden can be reached at ground level. On the hillside, the living area forms a spatial unit with a fan-shaped, enclosed inner courtyard. As a contemplative element, the courtyard complements the interior, allowing winter light to penetrate deep into the building. The tree in the middle protects against excessive sunlight in summer. Private retreats for residents are located on the lower floor.

The living area is made of wood and rests on a massive plinth dug into the slope and made of exposed concrete; it is clad with silver fir slats. Only at second glance can the different degrees of transparency be seen from the outside. On the inside, however, a lively diversity unfolds through the interplay of openness and unity, light and shadow. The reduced materialization inside creates calm clarity: silver fir paneling on the outer walls and on the ceiling, in combination with white dividing elements inside, contrasts with the solid oak floorboards.

Geothermal energy is used to heat the house, which has a low heating requirement. The ecological energy concept is supplemented by a storage heater in the living area, controlled ventilation, and a photovoltaic system that covers the building's electricity needs. The holistic building concept included the use of the most natural building materials possible from renewable raw materials, the use of highly skilled local craftsmen, as well as redensification in an already developed environment.

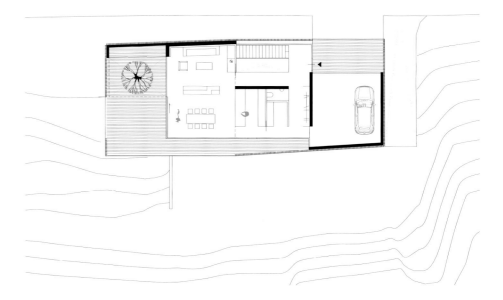

Floor plan, first floor

The glass facade of the living area opens onto the landscape and the surrounding deck terrace. An opening in the roof and the rear wall give the back of the terrace the feel of an intimate courtyard.

Biographies

Mona Bayr

born 1976 in Schwäbisch Gmünd, Germany
studied architecture in Augsburg, Germany, as well as at the University of Applied Arts Vienna, where she completed her master's degree in 2007, and in the design studios of Zaha Hadid, Greg Lynn, and Wolf Dieter Prix. Since 2011, she has been working towards her doctorate at the University of Applied Arts Vienna. Mona Bayr has worked in various architectural offices in Austria and abroad, including Coop Himmlb(l)au in Vienna from 2001 to 2015, where she was project manager for the Musée des Confluences in Lyon and the Museum of Contemporary Art in Shenzhen. In 2004 she founded her own office, the Atelier H$_2$A. Since 2017, she is a professor at HTWG Konstanz.
www.H-2-A.com

Lina Bo Bardi

born 1914 in Rome, Italy
died 1992 in São Paulo, Brazil
graduated in architecture from the Sapienza in Rome, moved to Milan in 1940, where she worked in the office of Gio Ponti and for the magazines *Domus* and *Lo Stile*. In 1946 she married the gallery owner and art critic Pietro Bardi and emigrated with him to Brazil. There she designed the Glass House and the sensational Museu de Arte de São Paulo (MASP). With her interest in folk art, she promoted Brazilian identity, founding the Museu de Arte Popular in Salvador da Bahía in 1960. Lina Bo Bardi is considered one of the most important architectural voices of Brazilian post-war modernism.

Dirk Boll

born 1970 in Kassel, Germany
studied law and cultural management in Freiburg and Ludwigsburg and received his doctorate on the organizational forms of the art market. He has been working for the British auction house Christie's since 1998 and has been President of Christie's Europe, Middle East, Russia, and India (EMERI) since 2017. Dirk Boll is Professor at the Institute for Cultural Management and Media Management at the University of Music and Theater Hamburg and has published numerous articles and books on the legal and economic foundations of the art market and its players.

Sol Camacho

born 1981 in Mexico City, Mexico
studied architecture and urban design and works at the interface between practice and research. In 2011, she co-founded the architectural practice RADDAR in São Paulo, which was awarded the silver medal of the Regional Lafarge Holcim Awards 2017 Latin America in 2017. In 2018, she curated the Brazilian pavilion *Walls of Air* at the Venice Architecture Biennale. Since 2017, Sol Camacho has been director of the Instituto Bardi/Casa de Vidro, where she is responsible for exhibitions and cultural events and coordinates Lina Bo Bardi's archive.
www.raddar.org

Beatriz Colomina

born 1952 in Madrid, Spain
is an architectural historian and theorist. Since 1988 she has been Professor of History and Theory at Princeton University School of Architecture, where she founded the Media and Modernity program and directs the graduate and doctoral programs. She is a visiting professor at the Städelschule in Frankfurt and author of *X-Ray Architecture* (2019), *Domesticity at War* (2007), and *Sexuality and Space* (1992), among others. In 2020 she was awarded the Ada Louise Huxtable Prize of the W Awards for her theoretical work.

Odile Decq

born 1955 in Laval, France
studied architecture and urban planning in Paris. Together with Benoît Cornette, she opened the architectural office ODBC in 1985. Since his death in 1998 she has run it alone, today under the name Studio Odile Decq. After teaching for many years at the École Speciale d'Architecture Paris (ESA), she founded the alternative architecture school Confluence Institute for Innovation and Creative Strategies in Architecture in 2013. Odile Decq has received numerous awards throughout her career, including the Golden Lion (1996) and the Jane Drew Prize (2016). In addition to her work as an architect, she is committed to inclusiveness and the visibility of women in architecture; among other things, this commitment has led to her participation in a flash mob at the 2018 Venice Architecture Biennale.
www.odiledecq.com

Elke Delugan-Meissl

born 1959 in Linz, Austria
studied at the Faculty of Architecture at the University of Innsbruck and in 1993, together with Roman Delugan, founded the architectural office Delugan Meissl in Vienna, which was expanded to Delugan Meissl Associated Architects (DMAA) in 2004. From 2010 to 2011 she taught at the University of Applied Arts Vienna. In 2015 Elke Delugan-Meissl received the Grand Austrian State Prize together with her office partner. With its residential and cultural buildings in Europe, the US, and Asia, the firm is considered one of the most important and internationally renowned architectural firms in Austria.
www.dmaa.at

Julie Eizenberg

born 1964, Australia
founded Koning Eizenberg Architecture (KEA) in 1981 together with Hank Koning in Santa Monica (US) after studying architecture in Melbourne and Berkeley. After teaching at the Harvard Graduate School of Design, University of California, Los Angeles (UCLA), Yale School of Architecture, and others, she has been a lecturer at the Southern California Institute of Architecture (SCI-Arc) since 2003. Her portfolio includes residential buildings and educational institutions. In 2012 the office partnership received the Gold Medal of the American Institute of Architecture (AIA) and in 2019 the Gold Medal of the Australian Institute of Architecture.
www.kearch.com

Manuelle Gautrand

born 1961 in Marseille, France
has been running her own architecture firm Manuelle Gautrand Architecture since 1991, with a focus on cultural, office, and residential buildings, after working for six years in various architectural offices in Paris. In addition to teaching, she has been president of the Académie d'Architecture since 2016. In 2007, Manuelle Gautrand was awarded the title Chevalier dans l'Ordre des Arts et des Lettres and in 2017 she won the American Architecture Prize with the Alésia cinema.
www.manuelle-gautrand.com

Dominique Gauzin-Müller

born 1960 in Vincennes, France
is an architect and architecture critic and teaches on the subject of sustainability at the École Nationale Supérieure d'Architecture de Strasbourg (ENSAS) and the University of Stuttgart. As Professor h.c. of the UNESCO-CRAterre Chair Earthen architectures, constructive cultures, and sustainable development in Grenoble, Dominique Gauzin-Müller initiated the architecture prize TERRA Award 2016, the world's first prize for modern earth architecture.

Annette Gigon

born 1959 in Herisau, Switzerland
completed her studies at ETH Zurich
and founded the architectural office
Annette Gigon/Mike Guyer Architekten
in Zurich together with Mike Guyer in
1989. In 2003 she was appointed a
member of the Berlin Academy of Arts.
After numerous international guest professorships, she has been Professor
of Architecture and Design at ETH Zurich
since 2012. Her projects include museum
buildings, residential projects, and office
buildings, including the much-
acclaimed Prime Tower in Zurich.
www.gigon-guyer.ch

Silvia Gmür

born 1939 in Zurich, Switzerland
studied architecture at ETH Zurich, founded her own office in Basel in 1972, and
was offered a guest professorship at ETH
Zurich in the nineteen-eighties. After
several years of collaboration with the
Swiss architect Livio Vacchini, she and her
son founded the office Silvia Gmür Reto
Gmür Architekten in Basel in 2005. In
their buildings they are particularly interested in the facade as a spatial layer, as
in the new building for the Bürgerspital
Solothurn. In 2011 she received the Prix
Meret Oppenheim.
www.gmuerarch.ch

Eileen Gray

born 1878 in Enniscorthy, Ireland
died 1976 in Paris, France
studied at the Slade School of Fine Art
in London from 1898 to 1902. In 1902
she traveled to Paris to attend classes at
the Académie Colarossi and the Académie
Julian. Two years later she moved to
Paris. She began her design career with
exclusive lacquer furniture, which was
influenced by the spirit of Art Nouveau
and Japonism. Around 1920 she met the
architect Jean Badovici and planned her
first house, E.1027 in Roquebrune on the
Côte d'Azur, for the two of them. After
they separated, she lived in seclusion in
Menton and later in Paris. It was not until
the end of the twentieth century that her
work was rediscovered and her significant
contribution to modern design and architecture was recognized.

Cristina Guedes

born 1964 in Macau, Portuguese
overseas province, today China
founded the office Menos é Mais Arqui-
tectos in Porto in 1994 together with
Francisco Vieira de Campos after having
completed her architecture studies in
Porto in 1991. Her works are characterized by a reduced architectural language
developed from their context. Guedes is a
visiting professor at the Accademia di
Architettura di Mendrisio. In 2017
Cristina Guedes and Francisco Vieira de
Campos were appointed International
Fellows at the Royal Institute of British
Architects (RIBA).
www.menosemais.com

Melkan Gürsel

born 1970 in Istanbul, Turkey
studied architecture in Istanbul and
Barcelona. Since 1995, she has been a
partner in Tabanlıoğlu Architects in Istanbul, a firm founded in 1990. Together
with the French artist Arik Levy she developed the installation *Transition; Warm/
Wet* at the London Design Festival 2015
and designed the Turkish Pavilion at
the London Design Biennale 2018. In
2013 and 2018 they were awarded the
Big Project Middle East Award.
www.tabanlioglu.com

Itsuko Hasegawa

born 1941 in Shizuoka, Japan
studied architecture at Kantō Gakuin
University in Yokohama and at the Tokyo
Institute of Technology and founded
her own office Itsuko Hasegawa Atelier
in Tokyo in 1979. The expressive formal
language of her buildings is rooted in
Hasegawa's early connections to Japanese Metabolists, including Kenzo Tange,
and in her work in the office of the Japanese architect Kazuo Shinohara. In 1986
she won the Design Award of the Architectural Institute of Japan (AIJ); in 1997
she became an honorary member of
the Royal Institute of British Architects
(RIBA), and in 2006 of the American
Institute of Architects (AIA). Most recently she won the Royal Academy Architecture Prize 2018.
www.ihasegawa.com

Anna Heringer

born 1977 in Rosenheim, Germany
studied architecture at the University of
Art and Design Linz and at the age of
nineteen did development work in Bangladesh. One year after graduating, she
founded her own architectural office in
2005, Studio Anna Heringer, which specializes in sustainable building with
bamboo and clay. Her diploma thesis,
the METI School in Rudrapur, India, was
built in 2005 and received the Aga Khan
Award for Architecture in 2007. In 2011
she received the Global Award for Sustainable Architecture. In addition to guest
professorships at ETH Zurich, UP Madrid,
TU Munich, and Harvard Graduate School
of Design, she co-initiated the "Laufen
Manifesto" in 2013, which outlines seven
principles for a humane design culture.
www.anna-heringer.com

Zaha Hadid

born 1950 in Baghdad, Iraq
died 2016 in Miami, US
studied mathematics before she turned
to architecture in 1972 and began her
architectural studies at the Architectural
Association (AA) in London. In 1980 she
founded her own architectural practice,
Zaha Hadid Architects, in London. She
became world famous for her experimental architecture, which she described
as fluid, kinetic, and parametric. As a
professor, she has taught at Columbia
University, Yale University, and the University of Applied Arts Vienna, among others.
She has received numerous awards,
including the Pritzker Architecture Prize
in 2004, the highest distinction in architecture. Since her death, the office has
been run by Patrik Schumacher and four
other partners.
www.zaha-hadid.com

Fabienne Hoelzel

born 1966 in Switzerland
studied at ETH Zurich and in the US
before working at Herzog & de Meuron
in Basel. Between 2010 and 2012, she
headed the planning team of the São
Paulo Urban Development Authority and
received an award for her slum upgrade
program from UN-Habitat. After her
return to Switzerland, she founded her
own architecture firm, Fabulous Urban,
in Zurich in 2013, which promotes urban
planning and development processes in
emerging and developing regions with
research-led projects. Since 2017 she
has been Professor of Urban Design at
the State Academy of Fine Arts Stuttgart.
www.fabulousurban.com

Helle Juul

born 1954 in Vester Hjermitslev, Denmark
studied architecture in Aarhus and
headed the Skala architecture gallery
in Copenhagen between 1984 and 1989.
In 1990, together with Flemming Frost,
she founded the office Juul Frost Arkitekter in Copenhagen, whose projects
range from large-scale urban development projects to educational, commercial,
and residential buildings. In 1994 Helle
Juul received her doctorate from the
Royal Danish Academy of Fine Arts
(KADK) on the subject of architectural
changes in time and space.
www.juulfrost.dk

Karla Kowalski

born 1941 in Beuthen, today Bytom,
Poland
studied architecture at the Technische
Hochschule Darmstadt and at the
Architectural Association (AA) in London.
While working at the office Behnisch &
Partner in Munich, she met Michael
Szyszkowitz, with whom she founded a
joint office in Graz in 1978, which is now
called Szyszkowitz-Kowalski + Partner.
Between 1988 and 2003 she was professor at the University of Stuttgart and
director of the Institute of Public Buildings and Design. She has been a member
of the Berlin Academy of Arts since 1993.
www.szy-kow.com

Anupama Kundoo

born 1967 in Pune, India
founded her application-oriented research
practice Anupama Kundoo Architects
in Auroville, India in 1990, which she now
runs from Berlin and Pondicherry, India.
With the help of materials research,
Anupama Kundoo Architects try to keep
an eye on the environmental impact and
ecological footprint of the users of their
residential and public buildings. In 2008,
she received a doctorate for her work
on the clay building pioneer Ray Meeker
from the Berlin Institute of Technology.
Following international teaching activities,
she has been Professor of Structural
Design at the University of Applied
Sciences Potsdam since 2018 and was
a visiting professor at Yale University
in spring 2020.
www.anupamakundoo.com

Anne Lacaton

born 1955 in in Saint-Pardoux-la-Rivière, France
studied architecture and urban planning in Bordeaux. In 1989 she co-founded the architectural office Lacaton & Vassal in Paris together with Jean-Philippe Vassal, which she still runs with him today. Her work focuses on the conversion of social housing estates of postwar modernism. She taught at the University of Madrid, École Polytechnique de Lausanne (EPFL), and Harvard Graduate School of Design, and has been Professor of Architecture and Design at ETH Zurich since 2017. In 2019 Lacaton & Vassal, together with the participating architectural firms Frédéric Druot Architecture and Christophe Hutin Architecture, received the Mies van der Rohe Award for the Grand Parc Bordeaux conversion project.
www.lacatonvassal.com

Regine Leibinger

born 1963 in Stuttgart, Germany
founded the firm Barkow Leibinger in Berlin together with Frank Barkow in 1993 after studying architecture in Berlin and at Harvard. With a focus on buildings for production, logistics, and administration, her special interest lies in experimental materials research and digital fabrication techniques. She has taught at the Architectural Association (AA) and Princeton University, among others, and was most recently Professor of Construction and Design at the Berlin Institute of Technology. She has been a member of the Academy of Arts in Berlin since 2016 and was appointed honorary member of the American Institute of Architects (AIA) in 2020.
www.barkowleibinger.com

Lu Wenyu

born 1966 in China
studied architecture at Nanjing Institute of Technology, where she met her future office partner and husband Wang Shu. In 1998 they founded the Amateur Architecture Studio in Hangzhou. In their designs, the duo takes up local craft traditions and brings them into harmony with contemporary design. They use and recycle traditional materials such as bamboo, wood, and brick. In 2010 both received the Schelling Architecture Award. The 2012 Pritzker Architecture Prize was awarded exclusively to partner Wang Shu.

Dorte Mandrup

born 1961 in Aarhus, Denmark
studied architecture in Aarhus and sculpture and ceramics in the US. In 1996 she co-founded the studio Fuglsang & Mandrup-Poulsen and three years later founded her own architectural office Dorte Mandrup in Copenhagen. In her sculptural buildings, she places particular emphasis on close interaction between architecture, environment, and the needs of the users. She is Vice President of the Louisiana Museum of Modern Art and Professor at the Royal Danish Academy of Fine Arts (KADK). She has received numerous awards, most recently winning the 2019 Berlin Art Prize in the Architecture Section.
www.dortemandrup.dk

Rozana Montiel

born 1962 in Mexico City, Mexico
studied architecture, urban planning, and architectural theory in Mexico City and Barcelona before founding her own office, Rozana Montiel Estudio de Arquitectura, in Mexico City. Her projects are often located in public space and show her deep interest in vernacular building methods. In 2010 and 2013 she was the first woman to receive two scholarships from the National Fund for Culture and the Arts (FONCA). Most recently, she received the Global Award for Sustainable Architecture in 2019.
www.rozanamontiel.com

Kathrin Moore

born in Germany
studied architecture in Hannover and urban planning at Yale University in the US. From 1972 she worked for over twenty years as a partner and Director of Urban Design and Planning at Skidmore, Owings & Merrill (SOM), until she founded her own firm, MooreUrban Design in 2000, which has been developing spatial strategies and master plans for areas and cities around the world. In addition to her activities in public bodies, juries, and committees, she has been a member of the San Francisco Planning Commission since 2006 and is thus jointly responsible for the supervision and implementation of all planning projects in the city. In 2017 she became a Fellow at the American Institute of Certified Planners (AICP) College, the prestigious US institute for urban planners.

Farshid Moussavi

born 1965 in Shiraz, Iran
emigrated with her family to Great Britain in 1979, where she studied architecture before going to the US for her master's degree at the Harvard Graduate School of Design. In 1993 she founded the Foreign Office Architects (FOA) with her husband Alejandro Zaera-Polo. Since their separation in 2011 she has run her own office, Farshid Moussavi Architecture (FMA), in London. After teaching at the Architectural Association (AA) in London and the Academy of Fine Arts Vienna, she has been a professor at the Harvard Graduate School of Design since 2006. She is a columnist for the *Architectural Review* and her research at the university has resulted in three publications to date, *The Function of Ornament* (2006), *The Function of Form* (2009), and *The Function of Style* (2015).
www.farshidmoussavi.com

Carme Pinós

born 1954 in Barcelona, Spain
studied architecture and urbanism in Barcelona. In 1982 she founded an architectural office with her then husband Enric Miralles, and since their separation in 1991 she runs her own architectural office, Estudio Carme Pinós, in Barcelona. Her work ranges from urban planning projects to furniture design. As a visiting professor, she has taught at the Columbia University Graduate School of Architecture, Planning, and Preservation, Harvard Graduate School of Design, and the Accademia di Architettura di Mendrisio. In 2016 Carme Pinós received the Richard J. Neutra Medal for Professional Excellence and in 2018 she was appointed Berkeley-Rupp Professor at the College of Environmental Design in California.
www.cpinos.com

Nili Portugali

born 1948 in Haifa, Israel
studied architecture at the Architectural Association (AA) in London, followed by postgraduate studies in architecture and Buddhism in Berkeley, US, at the chair of Christopher Alexander, with whom she later worked in his Center for Environmental Structure. In 1979 she founded her own studio, Nili Portugali Architect. In her architectural projects she follows a holistic-phenomenological approach, which she also addressed as director and screenwriter of the feature film *And the Alley She Whitewashed in Light Blue* (2019). She taught at the Technion in Haifa and at the Bezalel Academy of Arts and Design in Jerusalem.
www.niliportugali.com

Paula Santos

born 1961 in Porto, Portugal
studied architecture in Porto. After working with Carlos Guimarães and Luís Soares Carneiro (CG+LSC) and Eduardo Souto de Moura, among others, she founded her own office, Paula Santos Arquitectura, in 2000, focusing on residential construction. For the Pavilion of the Future for Expo '98 in Lisbon, Santos designed a temporary pavilion together with Rui Ramos and Miguel Guedes that received the Portuguese Order of Merit.
www.paulasantosarq.com

Patrik Schumacher

born 1961 in Bonn, Germany
has been an architect and partner of Zaha Hadid Architects since 2002. His studies in philosophy and mathematics were followed by the study of architecture in Stuttgart and London. During his studies in London he did an internship with Zaha Hadid in 1983, and since 1988 he has worked regularly in her architecture office. Schumacher is regarded as the theoretical mastermind of parametrism, the basis of which is the consistent use of digital design techniques. He teaches at the University of Innsbruck, is co-director of the Design Research Laboratory of the Architectural Association (AA) in London, and a member of the Royal Institute of British Architects (RIBA) and the Academy of Arts in Berlin.
www.patrikschumacher.com

Ursula Schwitalla

born 1948 in Heidelberg, Germany
studied history, geography, politics, and art history and works as an exhibition curator and art consultant. Her doctorate on the Cistercian Abbey of Bebenhausen was followed by her work at the Collaborative Research Center for the Middle East at the University of Tübingen and various teaching positions in geography and art history. As chairwoman of the Tübinger Kunstgeschichtliche Gesellschaft e.V., lecturer, and extraordinary member of the Association of German Architects (BDA), she has been responsible for the lecture series "Architecture Today" at the University of Tübingen for twenty years, which has resulted in publications such as *Built or Unbuilt: Architects Present Their Favourite Projects* (2006) as well as the present book.

Kazuyo Sejima

born 1953 in Hitachi, Japan
gained her first experience as a graduate architect in 1981 as an employee of Toyo Ito after graduating from Nihon Joshi Daigaku, a Japanese private university for women. Six years later, she founded her own architectural office, Kazuyo Sejima & Associates, in Tokyo and has since developed an unmistakable minimalist architectural language of dissolution and fragility, in which she mainly uses the materials exposed concrete, steel, aluminum, and glass. Since 1995, she has run the office together with Ryūe Nishizawa under the name SANAA. In 2010 she was the first woman to be curator of the Architecture Biennale in Venice, and in the same year she was the second woman to receive the Pritzker Architecture Prize together with her office partner Nishizawa.
www.sanaa.co.jp

Annabelle Selldorf

born 1960 in Cologne, Germany
studied architecture at the Pratt Institute in New York and at Syracuse University in Florence. In 1988 she founded her own firm, Selldorf Architects, in New York, which designs primarily cultural and residential buildings and interiors. She taught at the Harvard Graduate School of Design and is a member of the American Academy of Arts and Letters, whose Award in Architecture she received for her work in 2014. Under the name "Vica," she sells furniture based on her own designs and those of her father.
www.selldorf.com

Pavitra Sriprakash

born 1980 in Chennai, India
has been a partner in the architecture office Shilpa Architects, founded in Chennai by her mother Sheila Sriprakash, since 2008, after completing her architecture studies in India and the US. Her projects are based on vernacular design and construction practices and also take up philosophical themes of Indian culture. She is director and cofounder of the international architecture and urban planning firm SGBL Studio, based in Chicago, New York, and Seoul.
www.shilpaarchitects.com

Siv Helene Stangeland

born 1966 in Stavanger, Norway
studied French and art in Bordeaux before studying architecture. In 1996 she founded the office Helen & Hard in Stavanger, Norway, together with Reinhard Kropf from Graz. In their work, which they have summarized under the term "Relational Design," they develop alternative construction methods, drawing on local knowledge and resources such as the legacies of the timber construction or oil industries. In 2013 they were nominated for the Mies van der Rohe Award.
www.helenhard.no

Brigitte Sunder-Plassmann

born 1956 in Cloppenburg, Germany
studied Romance and German languages and literature as well as art history in Germany and France. She then worked as a journalist before founding the joint architectural office Sunder-Plassmann Architekten in Kappeln with Gregor Sunder-Plassmann in 1984, which specializes in cultural buildings. In 2014 they received the European Museum of the Year Award for the Museum of Innocence in Istanbul.
www.sunder-plassmann.com

Lene Tranberg

born 1956 in Copenhagen, Denmark
immediately after her architecture studies in Copenhagen, she founded the studio Lundgaard & Tranberg Arkitekter with Boje Lundgaard, which they ran together until 2004. Today she runs the studio together with sixteen partners. Their projects range from residential and cultural buildings to industrial buildings and urban development projects in which they develop typologies that emerge from the site and are tailored to the needs of the users. Lene Tranberg taught at the Royal Danish Academy of Fine Arts (KADK) and was a visiting professor at the University of Washington, Seattle. Among numerous awards, she and her team received the RIBA European Award for the Tietgen Dormitory in 2007.
www.ltarkitekter.dk

Billie Tsien

born 1949 in Ithaca, US
studied art and architecture at Yale University and the University of California, Los Angeles. In 1977 she began working with Tod Williams, with whom she founded the joint studio Tod Williams Billie Tsien Architects and Partners in New York in 1986. Her works mainly comprise public buildings, which she develops from the interior, from the requirements of the users. Together with Tod Williams she has taught at Cooper Union, Harvard Graduate School of Design, Cornell University, the University of Texas, City College of New York, and currently at Yale University, together with Andrew Benner. The firm's work has received numerous awards, most recently the Praemium Imperiale 2019 of the Japan Art Association in the category of architecture.
www.twbta.com

Elisa Valero

born 1951 in Ciudad Real, Spain
studied architecture in Spain before she went to Mexico to teach at the National Autonomous University of Mexico (UNAM). There she realized her first building contract, the renovation of the restaurant Los Manantiales by Félix Candela, an architectural icon of Mexico. In 1997 she founded her own architectural office, elisavalero, in Granada. After international guest professorships, she has been a professor at the Escuela Técnica Superior de Arquitectura in Granada since 2012. As an architect, Elisa Valero seeks solutions that enable functional buildings with limited resources. For this she received the Swiss Architectural Award in 2018.
www.elisavalero.com

Nathalie de Vries

born 1965 in Appingedam, the Netherlands
is co-founder and director of the interdisciplinary architecture and urban planning office MVRDV together with Winy Maas and Jacob van Rijs. From 2015 to 2019 she was president of the Royal Institute of Dutch Architects (BNA). Since 2019 she has been Professor of Architectural Design with a focus on public buildings at the Technical University of Delft, where she advocates the productive and transformative qualities of buildings. Recent projects include the award-winning Baltyk office tower in Poland, as well as residential projects in France, the US, and the Netherlands.
www.mvrdv.nl

Andrea Wandel

born 1963 in Saarbrücken, Germany
studied architecture in Kaiserslautern and Darmstadt and began working as an architect in the Wandel Hoefer Lorch office in 1994. In 2014 she founded Wandel Lorch Architekten in Darmstadt together with Wolfgang Lorch, specializing in sacral and museum architecture as well as building in existing structures. Andrea Wandel has been a professor at Trier University of Applied Sciences since 2011 and is a member of the Convention of Building Culture and the Design Advisory Board in Mainz. Most recently, she was awarded the Deutsche Ziegelpreis in the special category "Bauen im Bestand" (Building in Existing Structures) in 2019.
www.wandellorch.de

Helena Weber

born 1956 in Graz, Austria
studied music before she completed her architecture studies in Austria and Finland. After graduation she founded her own studio in Dornbirn, Austria. Since 2019, she has been managing the architecture office Berktold Weber Architekten in partnership with Philip Berktold and mainly realizes residential buildings, often using wood. In 2019 Helena Weber and her office partner were awarded the Vorarlberger Holzbaupreis for the Haus am Eulenwald.
www.berktold-weber.com

Emilie Winkelmann

born 1875 in Aken, Germany
died 1951 at Gut Hovedissen, Germany
was the first female architecture student in Germany to study architecture at the Königlich Technische Hochschule in Hannover—but only as a guest student, without being allowed to take the exam. She decided against a life with family and opened her own office in Berlin in 1907, which she successfully ran until the NSDAP seized power. In the course of her career, Emilie Winkelmann created numerous residential and commercial buildings for private clients and women's organizations. It was not until 1928 that she was accepted into the Association of German Architects (BDA).

Literature and Sources

ACSA, Association of Collegiate Schools of Architecture: www.acsa-arch.org (accessed September 7, 2020).

Adam, Peter. *Eileen Gray: Architect/Designer: A Biography.* 2nd ed. London, 2000.

Alofsin, Anthony. *Frank Lloyd Wright: The Lost Years.* Chicago, 1993.

Anscombe, Isabelle. *A Woman's Touch: Women in Design from 1860 to the Present Day.* London, 1984.

ARVHA, Association for Research about City and Housing: www.femmes-archi.org/en (accessed September 5, 2020).

Architektinnenhistorie: Zur Geschichte der Architektinnen und Designerinnen im 20. Jahrhundert; eine erste Zusammenstellung, edited by Günther, Sonja et. al. Berlin, 1987.

Attfield, Judy, and Pat Kirkham, eds. *A View from the Interior: Feminism, Women, and Design.* London, 1989.

BAK, Federal Chamber of German Architects: www.bak.de/eng (accessed September 7, 2020).

BAK, Federal Chamber of German Architects. "Studierende nach dem ersten angegebenen Studienfach." www.bak.de/w/files/bak/07-daten-und-fakten/ausbildung/studierende_architektur_bisws2019-2020.pdf (accessed November 30, 2020).

BAK, Federal Chamber of German Architects. "Architektenbefragungen." www.bak.de/architekten/wirtschaft-arbeitsmarkt/architektenbefragungen (accessed November 30, 2020). Baumeister 8. *Wo sind die Architektinnen?* Munich, 2017.

Beckel, Inge, and Gisela Vollmer. *Terraingewinn.* Bern, 2002.

Becker, Lynn. "Frank Lloyd Wright's Right-Hand Woman." *Repeat,* 2005. www.lynnbecker.com/repeat/Mahony/mahony.htm (accessed September 4, 2020).

Berkeley, Ellen Perry, ed. *Architecture: A Place for Women.* Washington, DC, 1989.

Birmingham, Elizabeth Joy. "Marion Mahony Griffin and The Magic of America: Recovery, Reaction, and Re-entrenchment in the Discourse of Architectural Studies." Iowa Research Commons, 2000. www.lib.dr.iastate.edu/rtd/12310 (accessed September 4, 2020).

Blumenthal, Max. "Jean Badovici 1893–1956" [obit]. In *Techniques et Architecture,* 16th series (November 1956).

Boutelle, Sarah Holmes. "An elusive Pioneer: Tracing the work of Julia Morgan." In *Architecture: A Place for Women,* edited by Ellen Perry Berkeley and Matilda McQuaid. Washington, DC, 1989.

Boutelle, Sarah Holmes. *Julia Morgan: Architect.* New York, 1988.

Carboncini, Anna. "Lina Bo Bardi Designer." In *Lina Bo Bardi: Giancarlo Palanti; Studio D'Arte Palma 1948–1951,* edited by Nina Yashar. Milan, 2018.

Coelho Sanches, Aline. "The Glass House: A Worksite for Continuous Experimentation." Text and research developed for the Conservation and Management Plan for Instituto Bardi, as part of the "Keeping It Modern" program funded by the Getty Foundation, 2019.

Colomina, Beatriz. "A House of Ill Repute: E1027." In "Architektur, die [fem.], Baukultur ist auchweiblich," special issue *archithese,* no. 2 (2016), pp. 21–27.

Desāī, Mādahvī. *Women Architects and Modernism in India: Narratives and Contemporary Practices.* Abingdon, 2016.

Dörhöfer, Kerstin. *Pionierinnen in der Architektur.* Tübingen, 2004.

Engelberg, Meinrad von. "Weder Handwerker und Ingenieur: Architektenwissen der Neuzeit." In *Macht des Wissens: Die Entstehung der modernen Wissensgesellschaft,* edited by Richard von Dülmen and Sina Rauschenbach, pp. 241–71. Cologne, 2004.

Erben, Dietrich. "Architektur als öffentliche Angelegenheit." In *Der Architekt: Geschichte und Gegenwart eines Berufsstandes,* edited by Winfried Nerdinger, p. 109. Munich, 2012.

Finnish Architecture Navigator: finnisharchitecture.fi (accessed September 7, 2020).

Frichot, Hélène. "Architecture and Feminisms: Ecologies, Economies, Technologies." In *Critiques: Critical Studies in Architectural Humanities.* London, 2017.

Friedman, Alice T. "Girl Talk: Marion Mahony Griffin, Frank Lloyd Wright, and the Oak Park Studio." *Places Journal,* June 2011. placesjournal.org/article/marion-mahony-griffin/?cn-reloaded=1 (accessed September 5, 2020).

Friedman, Alice T. *Women and the Making of the Modern House: A Social and Architectural History.* New Haven, CT, 2006.

Friedmann, Alice T. "Your Place or Mine? The Client's Contribution to Domestic Architecture." In *Women's Places: Architecture and Design 1860–1960,* edited by Brenda Martins and Penny Sparke, pp. 65–81. Abingdon, 2003.

Hall, Jane. *Breaking Ground: Architecture by Women.* London, 2019.

Hayes McAlonie, Kelly. *Louise Blanchard Bethune: Pioneering Woman of American Architecture,* 2020. www.pioneeringwomen.bwaf.org/louise-blanchard-bethune (accessed November 20, 2020).

Hoppe, Ilaria. "Plautilla Bricci, die erste Architektin: Zum Verhältnis von Architektur und Geschlecht im römischen Seicento." In *Frauen und Päpste: Zur Konstruktion von Weiblichkeit in Kunst und Urbanistik des römischen Seicento,* edited by Eckhard Leuschner and Iris Wenderholm, pp. 171–85. Berlin, 2016.

IAWA, International Archive of Women in Architecture: spec.lib.vt.edu/iawa (accessed September 5, 2020).

Jähnert, Gabriele, ed. *Zur Geschichte des Frauenstudiums und Wissenschaftlerinnenkarrieren an deutschen Universitäten.* Berlin, 2001.

Kaufmann, Hermann, Susanne Ihsen, and Paula-Irene Villa Braslavsky, eds. *Frauen in der Architektur: Vorstudie zur Entwicklung einer drittmittelfinanzierten Forschungsprojektes über fachkulturell relevante geschlechtergerechte Veränderung in der Architektur.* Munich, 2018. mediatum.ub.tum.de/doc/1519783/1519783.pdf (accessed September 5, 2020).

Kuhlmann, Dörte. *Raum, Macht und Differenz: Genderstudien in der Architektur.* Vienna, 2002.

Kullack, Tanja, ed. *Architecture: A Woman's Profession.* Berlin, 2011.

Lange, Alexandra. "Overlooked No More: Julia Morgan, Pioneering Female Architect" *The New York Times,* March 6, 2019.

Le Corbusier [Charles-Édouard Jeanneret]. *My Work.* Translated by James Palmer. Introduction by Maurice Jardot. London, 1960.

Leuschner, Eckhard, and Iris Wenderholm, eds. *Frauen und Päpste: Zur Konstruktion von Weiblichkeit in Kunst und Urbanistik des römischen Seicento.* Berlin, 2016.

Lira, José. *Warchavchik: fraturas da vanguarda.* São Paulo, 2011.

Lollobrigida, Consuelo. *Plautilla Bricci: Pictura et Architectura Celebris; L'architettrice del Barocco Romano.* Rome, 2017.

Lorenz, Clare. *Women in Architecture: A Contemporary Perspective.* New York, 1990.

Maasberg, Ute, and Regina Prinz. *Die Neuen kommen.* Dessau, 2002.

Madame Architect: www.madamearchitect.org (accessed September 8, 2020).

Mahony Griffin, Marion. *The Magic of America.* Online publication. Chicago, 2007 [1894]. archive.artic.edu/magicofamerica/ (accessed September 5, 2020).

Martins, Brenda, and Penny Sparke, eds. *Women's Places: Architecture and Design 1860–1960.* Abingdon, 2003.

Mazón, Patricia. Das akademische Bürgerrecht und die Zulassung von Frauen zu den deutschen Universitäten 1865-1914. In *Akademisches Bürgerrecht und Frauenstudium.* www.gender.hu-berlin.de/de/publikationen/gender-bulletin-broschueren/bulletintexte/texte-23/texte23pkt2.pdf/at_download/file (accessed August 29, 2020).

Millar, John. "The First Women Architects." *The Architects' Journal* 11, November 11, 2010. www.architectsjournal.co.uk/practice/culture/the-first-woman-architect (accessed September 5, 2020).

MoMoWo, Women's Creativity Since the Modern Movement: www.momowo.eu (accessed August 28, 2020).

Müller, Ulrike. *Bauhaus Frauen.* Munich, 2019.

N-ails e.V. Netzwerk von Architektinnen, Innenarchitektinnen, Landschaftsarchitektinnen und Stadtplanerinnen. www.n-ails.de (accessed September 5, 2020).

NCARB, National Council of Architectural Registration Boards: www.ncarb.org (accessed September 7, 2020).

Nerdinger, Winfried, ed. *Der Architekt: Geschichte und Gegenwart eines Berufsstandes.* 2 Vols. Munich, 2012.

Nochlin, Linda. "Why Haver There Been No Great Women Artists?" In *Women, Art, and Power,* pp. 145–78. New York, 1988.

Pepchinski, Mary, Christina Budde, Wolfgang Voigt, and Peter Cachola Schmal, eds. *Frau Architekt: Seit mehr 100 Jahren; Frauen im Architekturberuf.* Tübingen, 2017.

Polleross, Friedrich. "Von redenden Steinen und künstlich-erfundenen Architekturen." *Römische Historische Mitteilungen* 49 (2007), pp. 319–96.

Rackard, Nicky. "The 10 Most Overlooked Women in Architecture History." *ArchDaily*, November 5, 2019. www.archdaily.com/341730/zhe-10-most-overlooked-women-in-architecture-history/>ISSN0719-8884 (accessed August 28, 2020).

Rafi, Samir. "Le Corbusier et Les Femmes Femmes d'Alger." *Revue d'histoire et de civilisation du Maghreb* (January 1968), pp. 50–61.

Rebelarchitette: www.rebelarchitette.it (accessed August 28, 2020).

Ricon Baldessarini, Sonia. *Wie Frauen bauen*. Berlin, 2001.

Ruby, Ilka, and Andreas Ruby. *MVRDV Buildings*. Updated edition. Rotterdam, 2016.

Schaefer Horton, Inge. *Early Women Architects of the San Francisco Bay Area: The Lives and Work of Fifty Professionals, 1890–1951*. Jefferson, NC, 2010.

Schenk, Luciana Bongiovanni Martins, Ligía Teresa Paludetto, and André Tostes Graziano. "The Glass House and Its Garden: Inventory and Discoveries." In *Plano de Gestão e Conservação da Casa de Vidro*, edited by Renato Anelli. Unpublished. São Paulo, 2018. Text and research developed for the Conservation and Management Plan for Instituto Bardi, as part of the "Keeping It Modern" program funded by the Getty Foundation, 2019.

Schönfeld, Christiane, ed. *Practicing Modernity: Female Creativity in the Weimar Republic*. Würzburg, 2006.

Seražin, Helena, Emilia Garda, and Caterina Franchini, eds. *Women's Creativity Since the Modern Movement (1918–2018): Toward a New Perception and Reception*. Ljubljana, 2018. doi.org/10.3986/9789610501060 (accessed September 5, 2020).

Statista: de.statista.com/statistik/daten/studie/37278/umfrage/geschlechterverteilung-bei-architekten (accessed August 31, 2020).

Stead, Naomi. *Women, Practice, Architecture*. London, 2014.

Stratigakos, Despina. *Where Are the Women Architects?* Princeton, NJ, 2016.

Stratigakos, Despina. *A Women's Berlin: Building the Modern City*. Minneapolis, 2008.

Suominen-Kokkonen, Renja. *The Fringe of a Profession: Women as Architects in Finland from 1890s to the 1950s*. Helsinki, 1992.

Torre, Susana, ed. *Women in American Architecture: A Historic and Contemporary Perspective*. New York, 1977.

Van Zijl, Ida. "Die Entstehung des Rietveld-Schröder-Hauses." In *Rietveld-Schröder-Haus*. Utrecht, 2017.

Von Moos, Stanislaus. "Le Corbusier as Painter." *Oppositions: Le Corbusier 1933–1960*, pp. 89–107. Edited by Kenneth Frampton. Cambridge, MA, 1980.

Walker, Lynne and Elizabeth Darling, eds. *AA Women in Architecture: 1917–2017*. London, 2020.

Walker, Lynne. "Architecture and Reputation: Eileen Gray, Gender, and Modernism." In *Women's Places: Architecture and Design 1860–1960*, edited by Brenda Martins and Penny Sparke, pp. 82–105. Abingdon, 2003.

Walker, Lynne. *British Women in Architecture 1671–1951*. London, 1984.

Walker, Lynne, ed. *Drawing on Diversity: Women, Architecture, and Practice*. RIBA Heinz Gallery Vol. 55. London, 1997.

Walker, Lynne. "The Entry of Woman into the Architectural Profession in England." In *The Education of the Architect*, edited by Neil Bingham, pp. 39–46. London, 1993.

Wang, Wilfried, and Peter Adam, eds. *E.1027: Eileen Gray*. The O'Neil Ford Monograph Series Volume 7. The University of Texas at Austin, Center for American Architecture and Design, 2017.

Wensky, Margret. *Die Stellung der Frau in der stadtkölnischen Wirtschaft im Spätmittelalter*. Vienna and Cologne, 1980.

Winton, Alexandra Griffith. "'A Man's House Is His Art': The Walker Art Center's Idea House Project and the Marketing of Domestic Design 1941–1947." *Journal of Design History* 17, No. 4 (2004), pp. 377–96.

Wright, Gwendolyn. "On the Fringe of the Profession: Women in American Architecture." In *The Architect: Chapters in the History of a Profession*, edited by Spiro Kostof, pp. 280–308. Oxford, 1977.

Image Credits

pp. 54–59
Denise Scott Brown, photographer Robert Venturi, courtesy Venturi, Scott Brown, and Associates; ACSA diagram, redrawn by Dorothee Hahn, source Association of Collegiate Schools of Architecture, www.acsa-arch.org; diagram academic staff TU Munich, redrawn by Dorothee Hahn, source *Frauen in der Architektur, Vorstudie zur Entwicklung eines drittmittelfinanzierten Forschungsprojektes über fachkulturell relevante geschlechtergerechte Veränderung in der Architektur*, https://mediatum.ub.tum.de/doc/1519783/1519783.pdf, p. 13; diagram full- and part-time work and diagram career break, redrawn by Dorothee Hahn, source Federal Chamber of German Architects, salary survey 2015; Ryūe Nishizawa and Kazuyo Sejima © Takashi Okamoto/SANAA; Yvonne Farrell and Shelley McNamara, photographer Andrea Avezzù © Archivio Storico della Biennale di Venezia-ASAC; flashmob © Ursula Schwitalla; diagrams Women Architects World Map, redrawn by Dorothee Hahn, source Rebelarchitette, www.rebelarchitette.it

pp. 64–67
Portrait © Atelier H2A; plans © Atelier H2A; facade courtyard, facade lake, interior terrace © Tom Philippi for Solarlux GmbH; view from gallery © Dorothea Caven

pp. 68–71
Portrait © Franck Juery; plans © Odile Decq; project photography © Jinri & Zhu Jie

pp. 72–74
Portrait © Hubert Dimko; visualizations, plans © Delugan Meissl Asscociated Architects

pp. 76–79
Portrait © Eric Staudenmaier; plan © KoningEizenberg; project photography © Eric Staudenmaier

pp. 80–83
Portrait © Jean Harixcalde; plan © Manuelle Gautrand Architecture; facade by day, foyer © Luc Boegly; facade by night, movie theater © Guillaume Guerin

pp. 84–87
Portrait © Christian Scholz; plans © Gigon/Guyer; project photography © Thies Wachter

pp. 88–91
Portrait © Reto Gmür; plans © Silvia Gmür Reto Gmür; project photography © Reto Gmür

pp. 92–95
Portrait © Francisco Moura Relvas; plans © Menos é Mais; project photography © José Campos

pp. 96–99
Portrait © Emre Dorter; plans © Tabanlıoğlu Architects; project photography © Emre Dorter

pp. 100–03
Portrait, plans © Itsuko Hasegawa Atelier; project photography © Shigeru Ono

pp. 104–07
Portrait © Martin Rauch; general view © Dominique Gauzin-Müller; plans © Studio Anna Heringer; bamboo shell, core © Jenny Ji

pp. 108–11
Portrait © Marco Sieber; plans © Fabulous Urban; Makoko Hotspot with tanks, playing children play © Fabulous Urban; Makoko Hotspot with surroundings © Isi Etomi; woman at blue rain barrel © Fabienne Hoelzel

pp. 112–15
Portrait © Juul Frost Architects; plan © Juul Frost Architects; auditorium, Campus © Felix Gerlach; Campus square © Juul Frost Architects; ice floes © Line Stybe Vestergaard

pp. 116–19
Portrait © Stadt Graz/Thomas Fischer; external view © Jimmy Lunghammer; plans © Szyskowitz-Kowalski; courtyard © Werner Krug

pp. 120–23
Portrait © Naushad Ali; plans © Anupama Kundoo Architects; Biennale © Javier Callejas; Auroville © Sebastiano Giannesini; color tests, production © Anupama Kundoo; interior space © Javier Callejas

pp. 124–27
All pictures © Philippe Ruault; plans © Lacaton & Vassal Architectes

pp. 128–31
Portrait © Corinne Rose & Elke Selzle; plans © Barkow Leibinger; external view in the evening © Laurian Ghinitoiu; interior spaces, facade © Simon Menges

pp. 132–35
Portrait © Amateur Architecture Studio; plans © Amateur Architecture Studio; project photography © LV Hengzhong

pp. 136–39
Portrait © Espen Grønli; plans © Dorte Mandrup Arkitekter; project photography © Adam Mørk

pp. 140–43
Portrait © Nin Solis/Rozana Montiel Estudio de Arquitectura; visualization © Rozana Montiel Estudio de Arquitectura; project photography © Sandra Pereznieto

pp. 144–47
Portrait, plans, riverside pictures © MooreUrban Design

pp. 148–51
Portrait © Anne-Katrin Purkiss; plans © Farshid Moussavi Architecture; general view, balconies, surroundings © Stephen Gill; balcony with plants © Paul Phung

pp. 152–55
Portrait © Wayne Taylor; plans © Estudio Carme Pinós; project photography © Duccio Malagamba

pp. 156–59
All images © Nili Portugali

pp. 160–63
Portrait, plans © paula santos | arquitectura; project photography © Nelson Garrido

pp. 164–67
Portrait © Aiko Suzuki; plans © Kazuyo Sejima+Ryūe Nishizawa/SANAA; general view with lake © Alain Herzog; interior space © Kazuyo Sejima+Ryūe Nishizawa/SANAA; bottom view, patio © Jörg Schwitalla

pp. 168–71
Portrait © Brigitte Lacombe; plans © Selldorf Architects; external view, facade, stairwell © Jason Schmidt, courtesy Selldorf Architects; exhibition space © Jason Schmidt, © Judd Foundation, licensed by VAGA, New York, NY

pp. 172–75
Portrait © Amrit Sahasranamam; plans, project photography © Shilpa Architects

pp. 176–79
Portrait © Rune Hammerstad; plans, visualizations © Helen & Hard

pp. 180–83
Portrait © Johanna Sunder-Plassmann; plans © Sunder-Plassmann Architekten; project photography © Johanna Sunder-Plassmann

pp. 184–87
Portrait © Søren Solkjær; plans © Lundgaard & Tranberg Arkitekter; courtyard, staircase © Jens M. Lindhe; general view © Anders Sune Berg

pp. 188–91
Portrait © Taylor Jewell; project photography © Giles Ashford; plans © Tod Williams Billie Tsien Architects

pp. 192–95
Portrait © Fernando Alda; plans © elisavalero; project photography © Fernando Alda

pp. 196–99
Portrait © Barbra Verbij; plans © MVRDV; interior space © Jeroen Musch; retreat corner, facade construction, external view © Daria Scagliola

pp. 200–03
Portrait © Johanna Lorch; plans © Wandel Lorch Architekten; existing buildings, new building © Anton Schedlbauer; top floor © Norbert Miguletz

pp. 204–07
Portrait © Darko Todorovic; plan © Helena Weber; project photography © Adolf Bereuter

The editor and publisher have made every effort to locate all copyright holders. If anyone has been inadvertently overlooked, please contact the editor or the publisher. All other uncredited images are from the author's archive.

Colophon

Editor
Ursula Schwitalla

Copy editing and proofreading
Irene Schaudies, Sarah Trenker

Translation from the German
Donna Blagg, Alison Kirkland,
Steven Lindberg (pp. 11–27, 55–61)

Graphic design and typesetting
Sylvia Fröhlich

Project management
Dorothee Hahn

Production
Thomas Lemaître

Reproduction
DLG Graphic, Paris

Printing and binding
Printer Trento s.r.l.

Paper
Magno Plus Silk 150 g/m²

Published by
Hatje Cantz Verlag GmbH
Mommsenstraße 27
10629 Berlin
Germany
www.hatjecantz.com

A Ganske Publishing Group Company

ISBN 978-3-7757-4857-5

Cover illustration
Denise Scott Brown in Las Vegas, 1966
Photographer Robert Venturi
Courtesy Venturi, Scott Brown,
and Associates

This book was made possible thanks to

Bund Deutscher Architekten
Landesverband Baden-Württemberg BDA

BRAKEFORCE ONE

COPRO

NON NOBIS - STIFTUNG, Stuttgart
Werner Sobek

Ritter SPORT

Deutsche Stiftung Frauen- und Geschlechterforschung
German Foundation for Gender Studies

TKG Tübinger
Kunstgeschichtliche
Gesellschaft e.V.

Universitätsbund
Tübingen e. V.

WÜRTH HAUS RORSCHACH

Zaha Hadid Architects

Ingrid und Klaus Fischer

Reiner Hähle

Elham Najapour

Friedrich Oesterle

Brigitte und Hellmut Raff

Heinz Reschke

Jörg Schwitalla